Fun With Lines and Curves

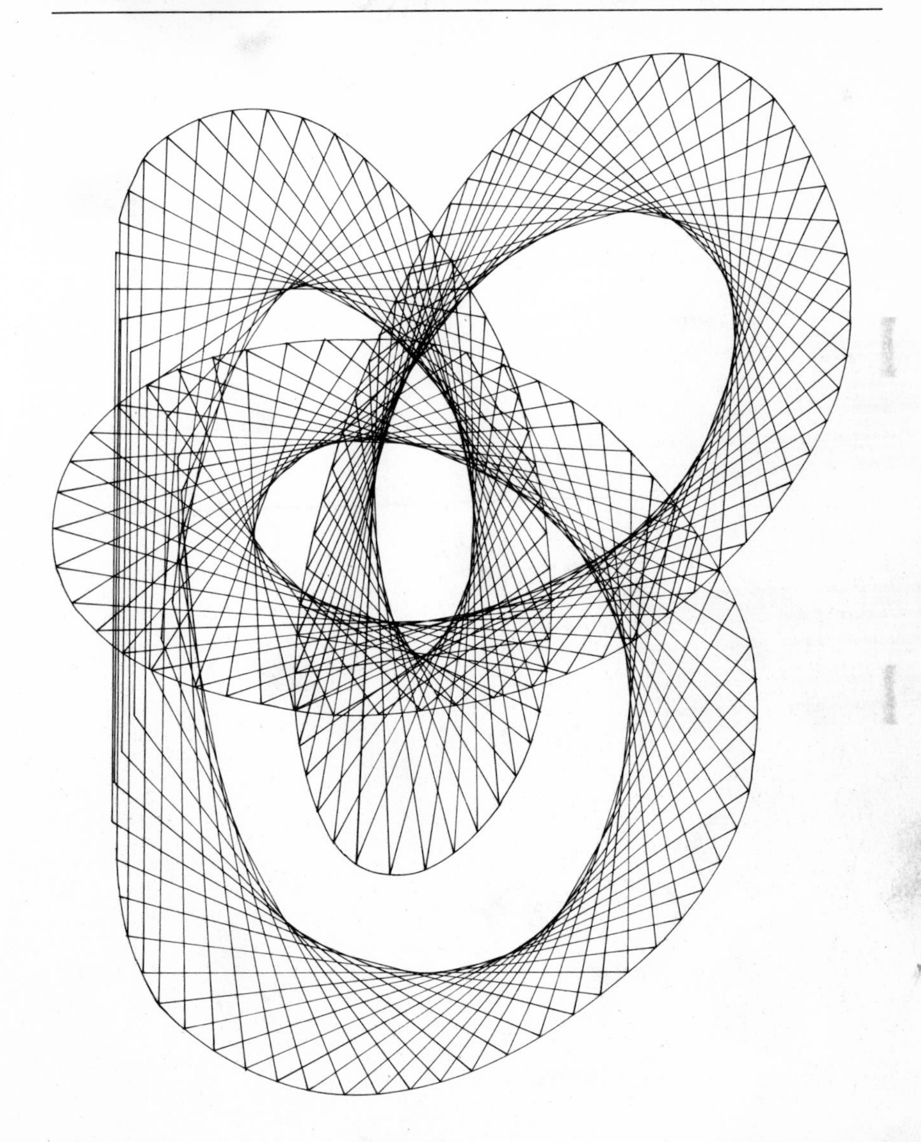

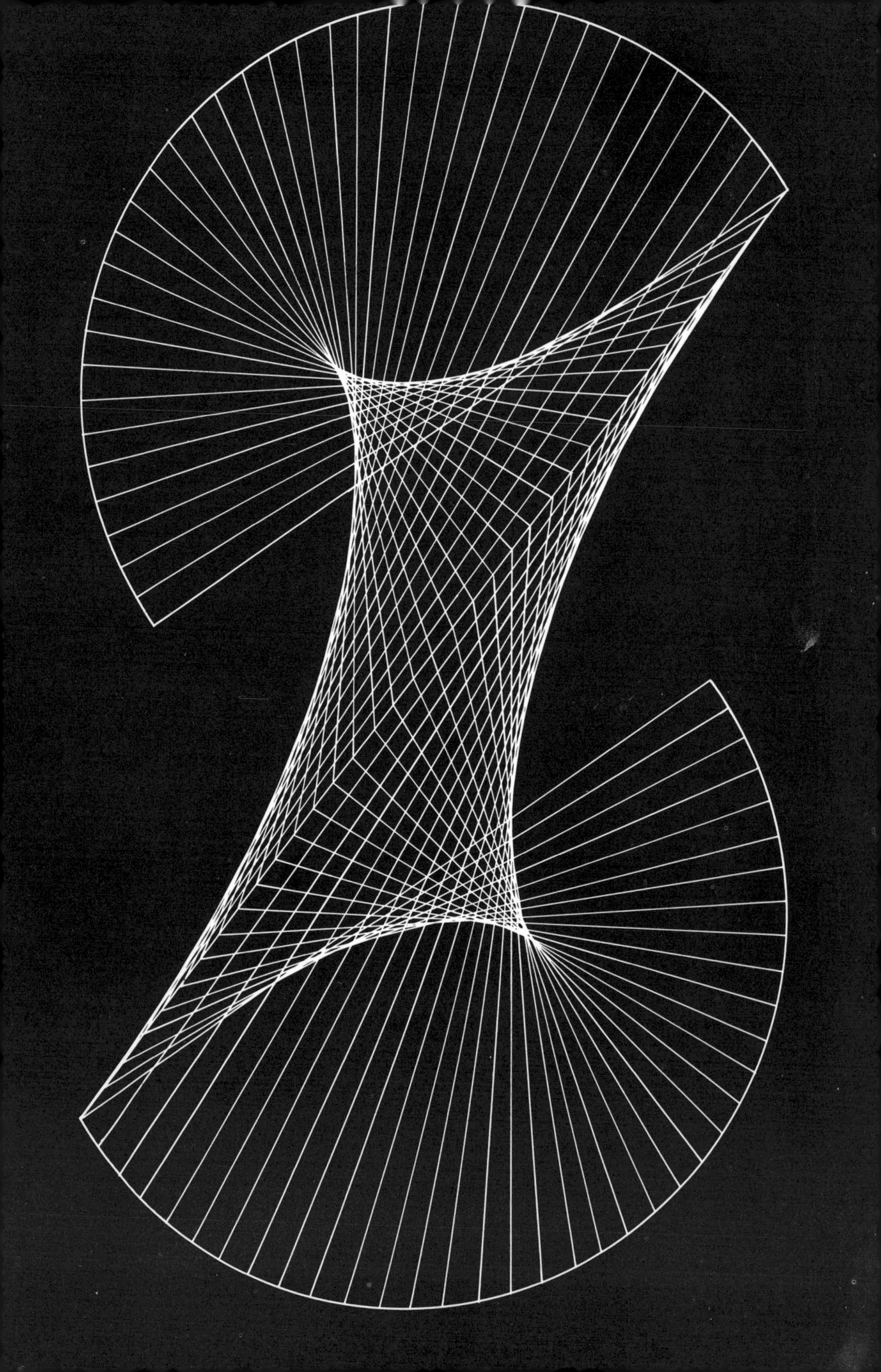

Elsie C. Ellison

FUN WITH LINES AND CURVES

With illustrations adapted from
the author's drawings by Susan Stan

Lothrop, Lee and Shepard Co.
New York

Library of Congress Cataloging in Publication Data

Ellison, Elsie C.
  Fun with lines and curves.

SUMMARY: Directions for geometric designs made with ruler, compass, and protractor and embellished with thread.
  1. Handicraft–Juvenile literature. 2. Geometrical drawing–Juvenile literature. [1. Geometrical drawing. 2. Handicraft] I.
TT160.E44   746.4   72-1095
ISBN 0-688-40012-4
ISBN 0-688-50012-9 (lib. bdg.)

Printed in the United States of America.

1 2 3 4 5 76 75 74 73 72

To
Mom and Dad
and
Ti Nibaca,
my reasons
for enjoying life
to the fullest

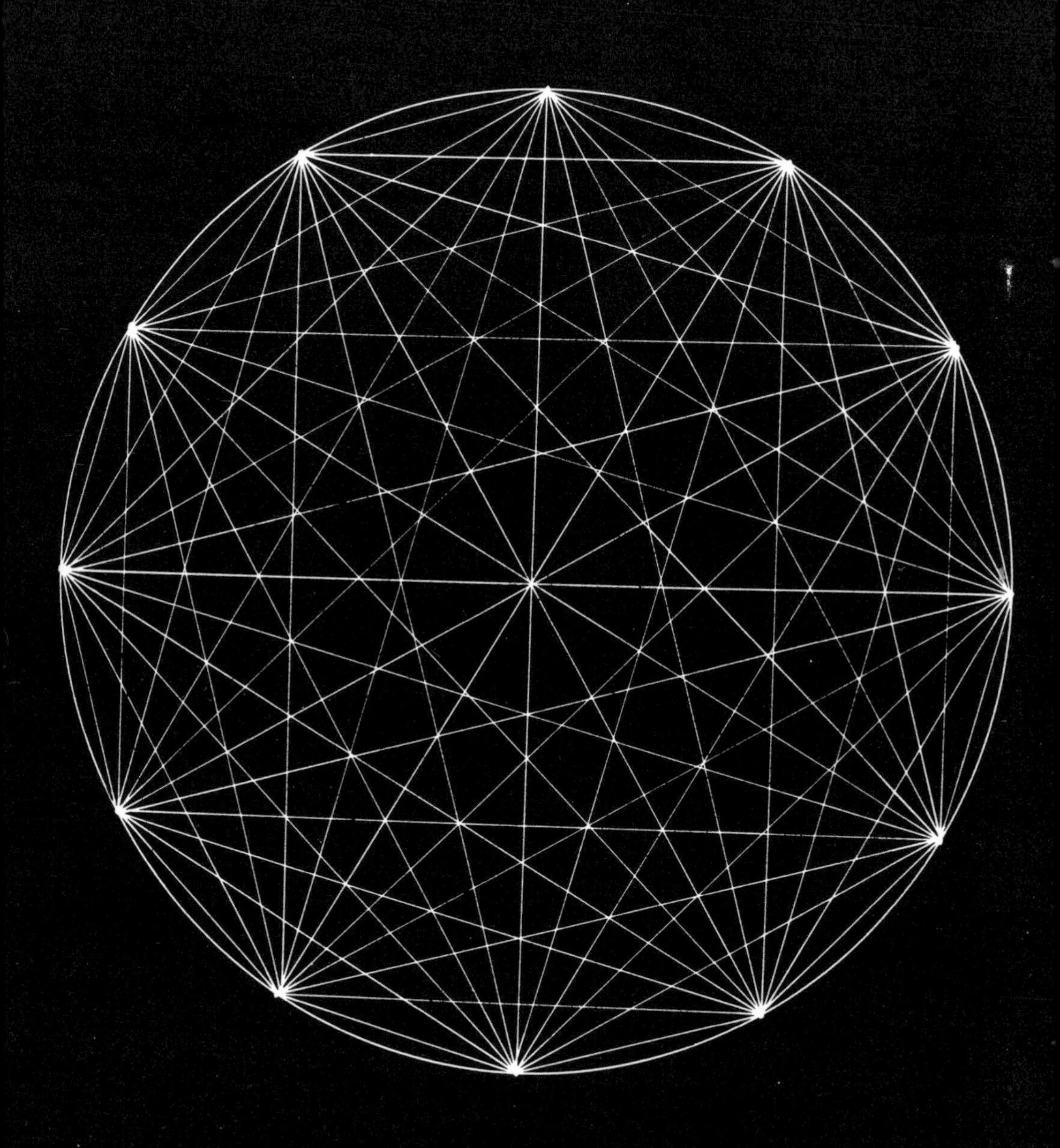

Contents

Foreword

If I said that by using this book you'd become a better student, it might scare some of you away; but if I said that you could become a more accurate student simply by having lots of fun, you might just buy that. Actually, that's exactly what can, and does, happen. Ask any one of two hundred students in the upper grades at Wilson Hill Elementary School in Worthington, Ohio. They didn't know at the time that their teacher was disturbed by their inability to use rulers accurately, and their teacher wasn't about to tell them so until they were completely wrapped up in a math project called *Fun With Lines and Curves.* They were hooked, the teacher saw great results, and the math class became the brightest spot of the day. This book follows the same plan used in the project. It was written so that other students (and teachers) might have the same kind of fun that the young people and their teacher had at Wilson Hill School.

The boys liked *Fun with Lines and Curves* as well as, or maybe better than, the girls. At first, when it was suggested that part of the equipment needed would be a needle and thread, the boys reneged. This was going to be "sissy stuff." Before the week was over, they had robbed their mothers' sewing baskets of so many spools of colored thread that the mothers were beginning to complain. After a class discussion, the boys decided to bargain with their mothers for the spools of thread. When all the beautiful designs made in the classroom and at home were displayed at a P.T.A. meeting, the parents, too, were hooked; and students began teaching Mom and Dad how to make their own designs. I have a strong feeling that thread sales went up considerably in the neighborhood stores. It can happen in your neighborhood, too, if you decide to try some of the ideas in *Fun With Lines and Curves.*

ELSIE C. ELLISON

Figure 1

Introduction

The first design you see was made by beginning with a cross-shaped starter (Figure 2). Many other designs can be made from the same starter by changing the position of the dots and the connecting lines.

The next two designs (pages 12 and 13) were made from a star-shaped starter (Figure 3). The design that is formed will depend upon the way the individual angles are worked.

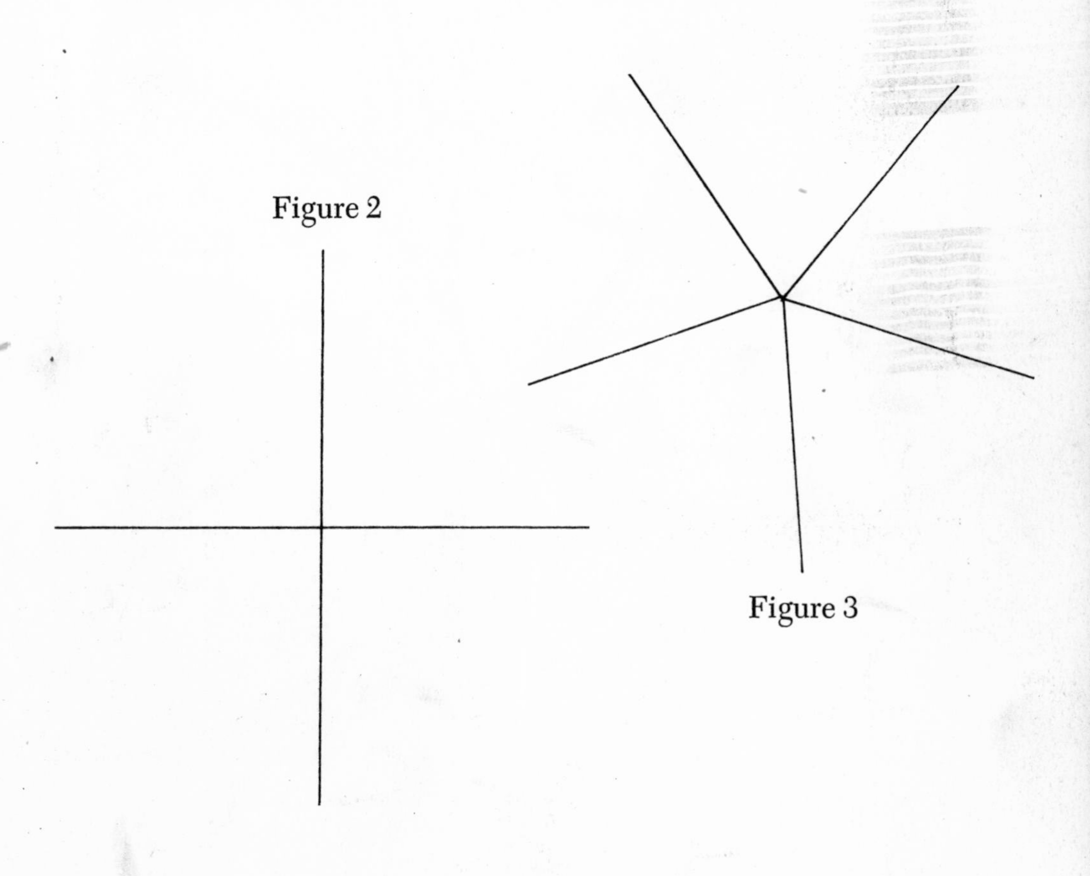

Figure 2

Figure 3

You can learn to make these three designs and many, many more by learning to use a ruler, a compass, and a protractor accurately and by following the few basic rules that are found on the following pages.

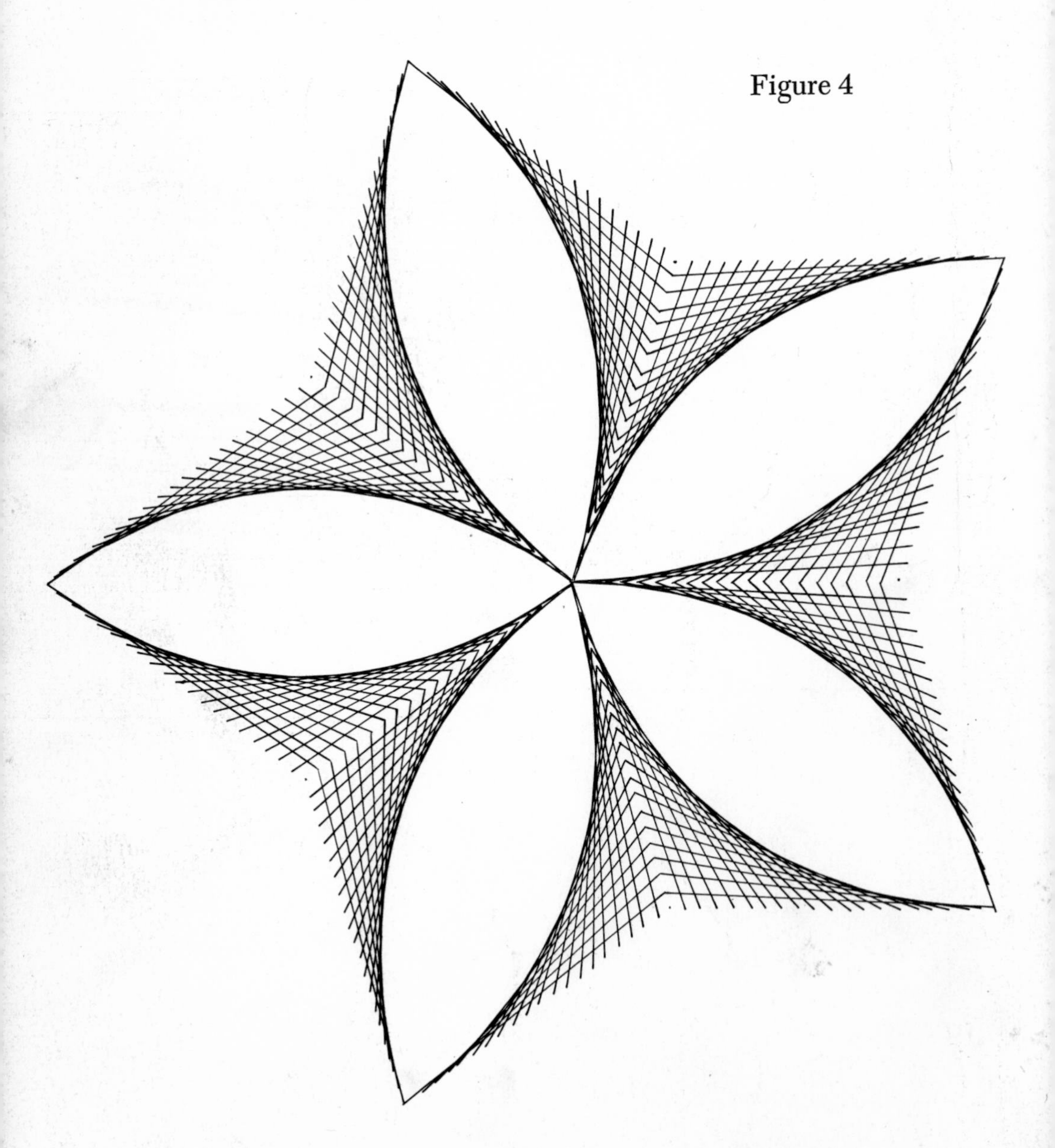

Figure 4

Figure 5

Tools

Since straight lines, curves, and angles are the bases for all the designs in this book, you will need a ruler, a compass, and a protractor. The better these three tools are, the more accurate your designs will be. You'll also need several sharp pencils; and you may want to get a small pencil sharpener—one that catches the shavings.

Ruler

A ruler will probably be your most often used tool. The 6-inch rulers in pencil boxes aren't quite long enough for most designs; a 12-inch ruler is much better. You'll use the ¼-inch measure more than any other, so if you need a new ruler it is best to buy the kind that has halves and fourths marked plainly instead of one that is cluttered with additional markings.

Compass

There are different kinds of compasses. Some attach to pencils (these are usually found in pencil boxes), and others have a screw adjustment where the two parts join. In the second type, one part has a sharp point and the other holds pencil lead. The one that just attaches to a pencil does not work quite so well as the other kind. However, either one is all right.

A compass is an easy tool to work with if you know the following:

1. The point of the compass is always the center of your circle. See A in Figure 2.

2. A straight line from one point on the circle through the center to the opposite point on the circle is called the diameter.

3. The radius is half the length of the diameter. It is the distance between the point and the pencil, or lead, part of your compass.

If you want a circle that is 4 inches in diameter, you must set your compass points at half that length—2 inches (radius).

Be sure to keep the point from moving as you swing the lead around in a circle.

If you work accurately, no one will know where the circle actually starts and where it ends.

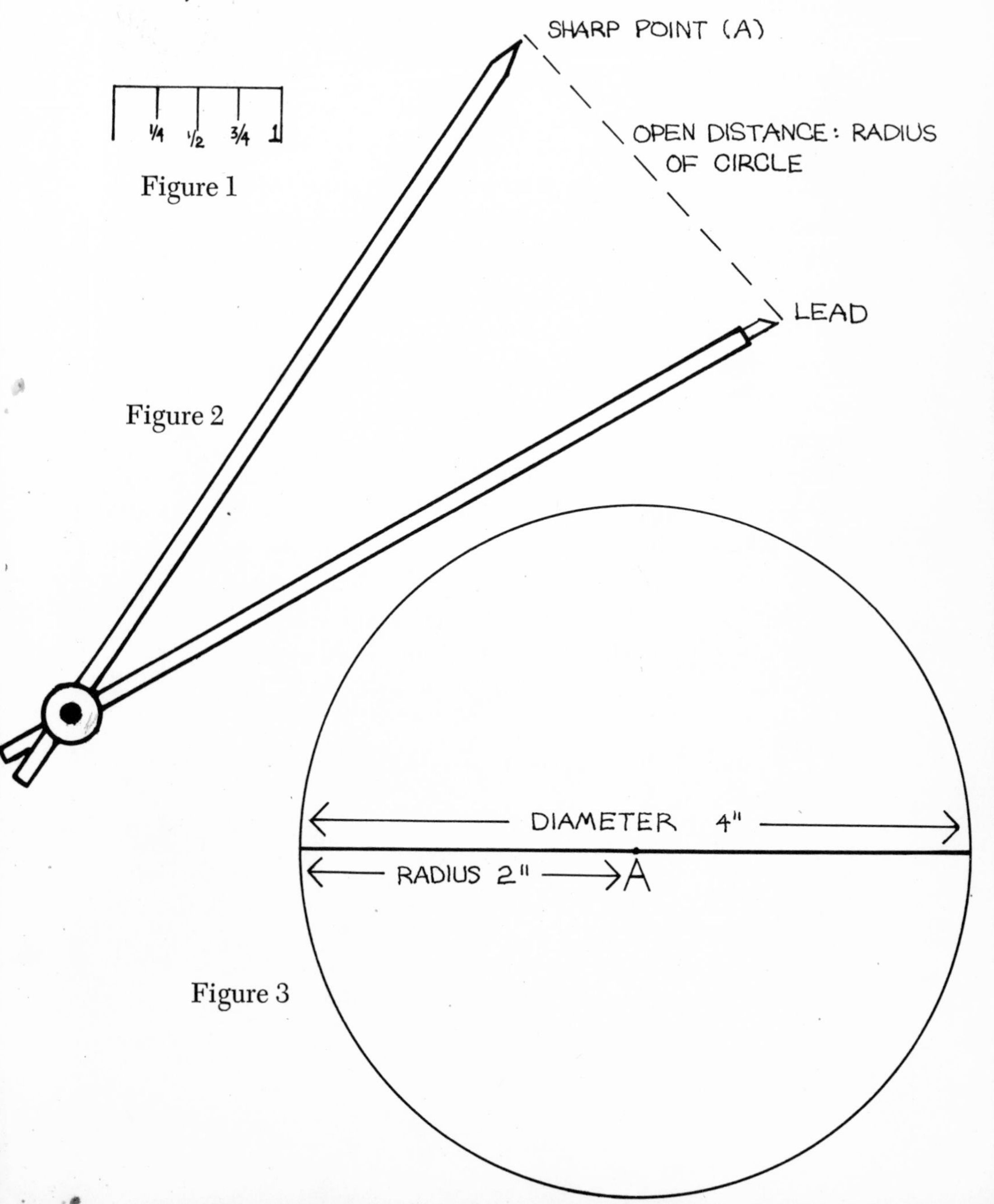

Figure 1

Figure 2

Figure 3

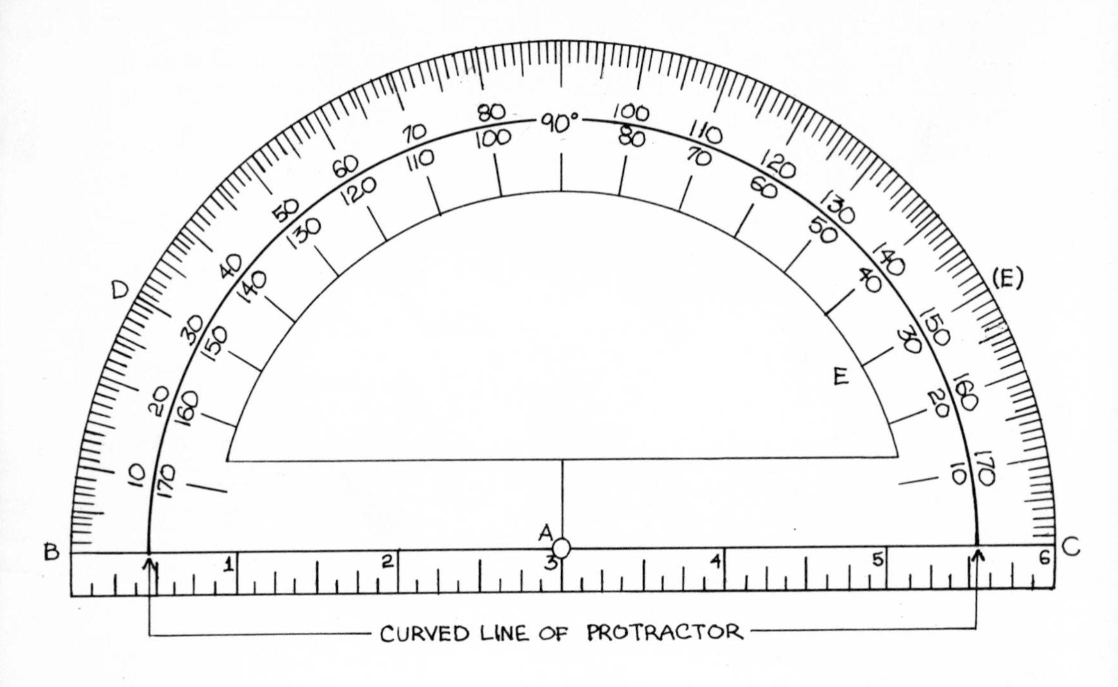

Figure 4

Protractor

Many pencil boxes have protractors in them. You may already have one; it looks like Figure 4.

A protractor is a little harder to learn to use than a ruler or a compass. Once you understand how to use it, you will be able to make angles of any size.

A simplified protractor, shown in Figure 4, has numerals on it to represent the number of degrees in a half-circle. Notice that there are also small markings between the numerals. Each marking represents 1 degree. Try making a 30-degree angle. Read each step, and do it before going on to the next step.

1. Draw a straight line 6 inches long and put a dot at the halfway point (3 inches). There is only one accurate way to get a dot exactly where you want it. Hold your pencil—a sharp one—straight up at the place where you want the mark. Twist the pencil between your fingers to make the dot.

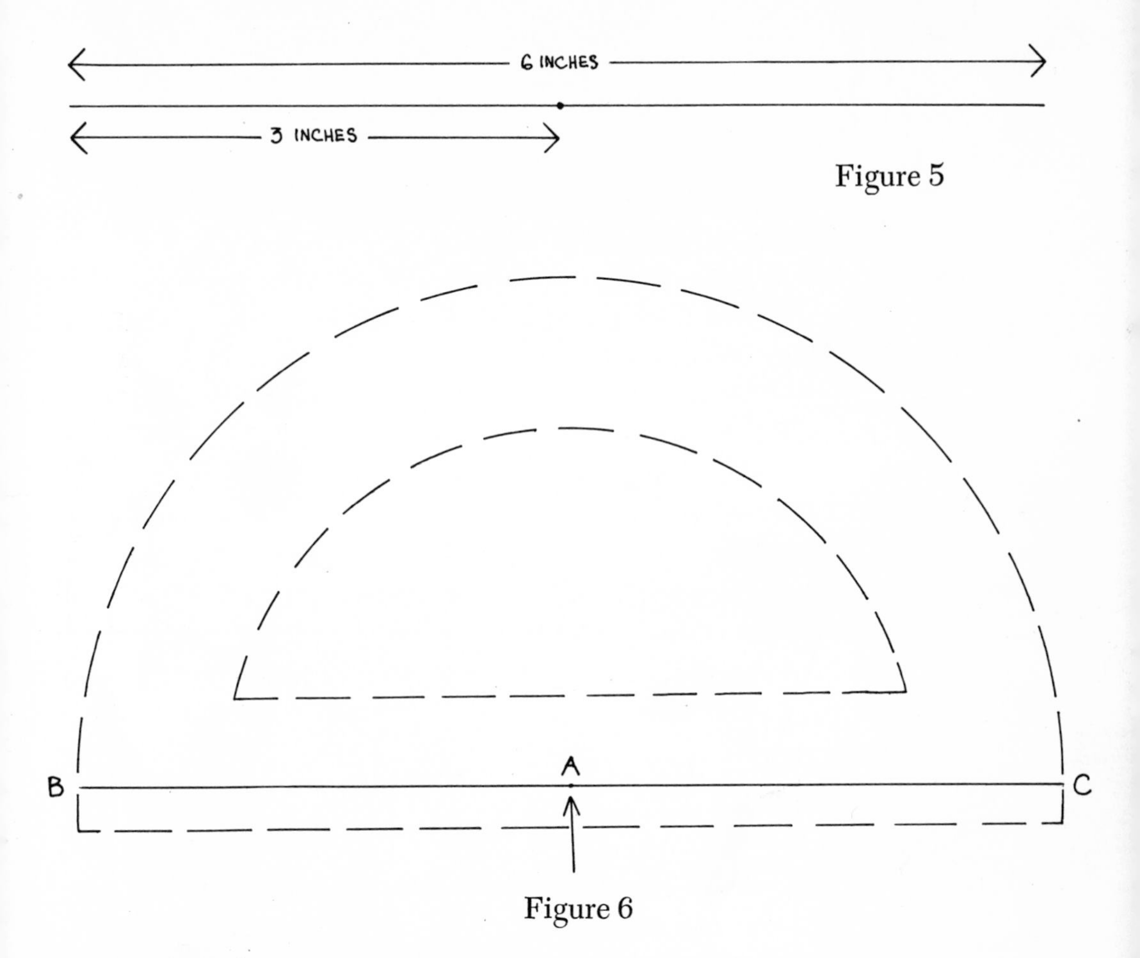

Figure 5

Figure 6

2. Lay your protractor along the line so that the hole of the protractor (A in Figure 6) is exactly over the dot, at 3 inches, and the line (BC) near the bottom of the protractor is over the line you drew on your paper.

In Figure 6, the unbroken line is the line you drew. The dot (arrow) is your halfway mark. The broken line is the protractor as it lies over your line. The line should be covered by the line on the protractor (BC), and you should be able to see your dot through the little hole (A) in the protractor.

3. Holding your protractor firmly so that it doesn't slip, put a dot where the line marked 30 ends on the outer curved part of the protractor (D in Figure 4 and Figure 7, on next page).

4. Remove the protractor. Using your ruler, carefully connect dot A on your line with the one you just made (D). You now have a 30-degree angle. The other angle is 150 degrees, since a straight line is a 180-degree angle.

If you want your 30-degree angle to go the other way, use the numeral 30 on the *right* side of the protractor, and put a dot where that 30-degree line ends on the *inner* curved part of the protractor (E in Figures 4 and 8). Then connect the two dots (A and E). Now your 150-degree angle is on the left side. If you want the angles under the line, turn the protractor around so that the curved part is below the line and proceed as you did with the other angles. Follow Figures 9 and 10 if you want to make your angles below the straight line.

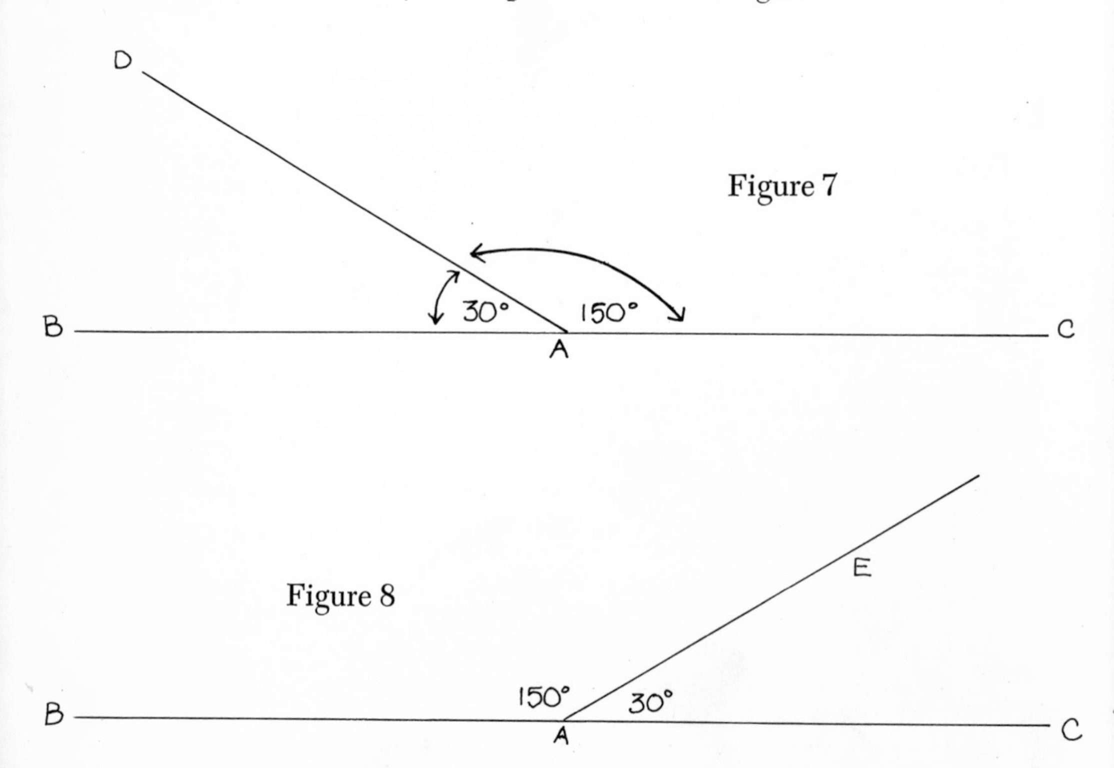

Figure 7

Figure 8

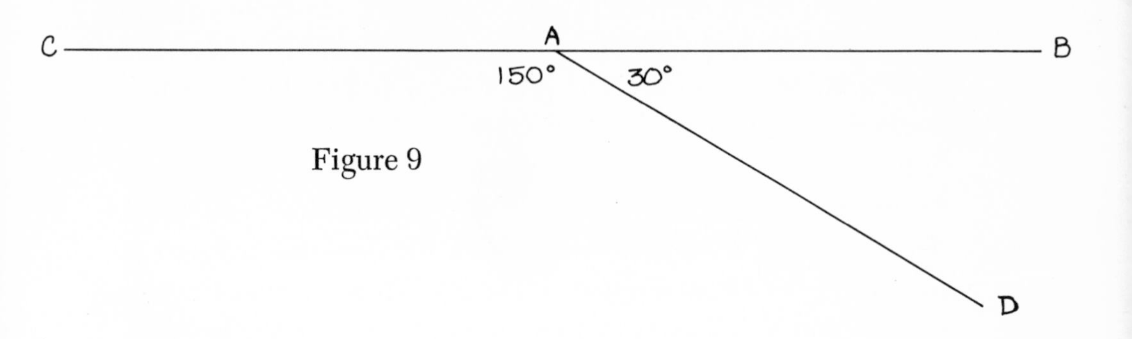

Figure 9

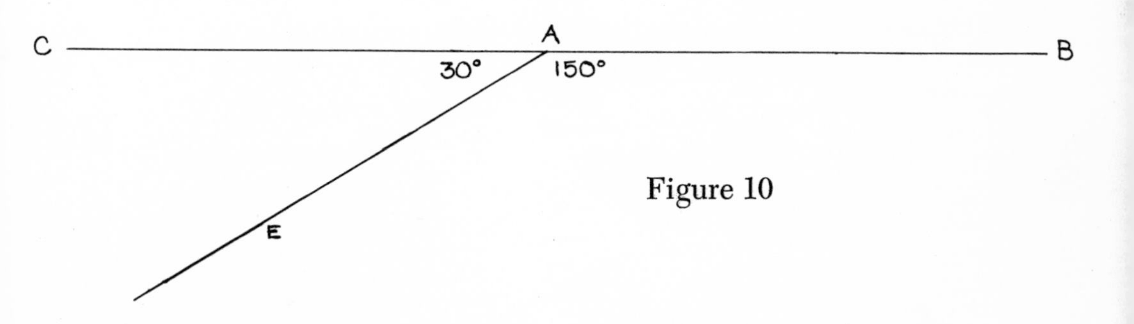

Figure 10

You can make a 72-degree angle as easily as you can make a 30- or a 70-degree angle. Instead of putting your dot at the line marked 70 degrees, move over two small lines and put it there. When you connect your dots, you will have a 72-degree angle.

Sometimes you will want your angle at the end of a line rather than at the midpoint. Here's how to do it:

1. Draw a line and put a dot at the end of the line where you want the angle to be.

2. Lay your protractor down so that the dot shows in the hole marked A in Figure 4 on page 16.

3. Align your line with BC on the protractor.
4. If your dot is at the right end of the line, use the numerals above the curved line of the protractor to measure the angle, but if it is at the left end, use the numerals under the curved line.
5. Remove the protractor and connect the dots. You now have one angle, not two angles on a straight line.

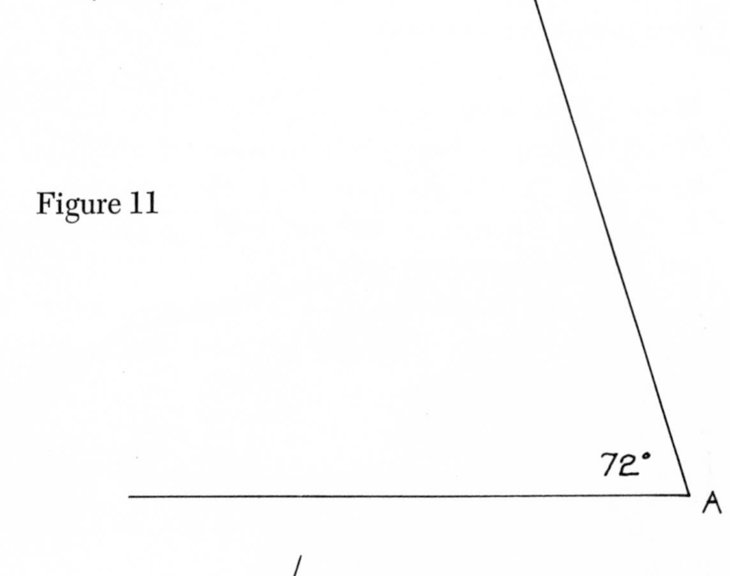

Figure 11

Figure 12

Making Polygons

A circle has a 360-degree angle at its center. If you divide 360-degrees into equal parts, you can make a polygon, such as a pentagon (five sides), a hexagon (six sides), or an octagon (eight sides). The shape of the polygon will depend upon the size of the angles at the center. You can make one with just your protractor and ruler.

Making a Hexagon

When making a hexagon, remember to read one step at a time; then do it before going on to the next step.

1. Draw a 3-inch line and put a dot at the *left* end. Be accurate and use a sharp pencil.

2. With your protractor mark a 60-degree angle. Remember that when the dot is at the left end, you use the numerals under the curved line.

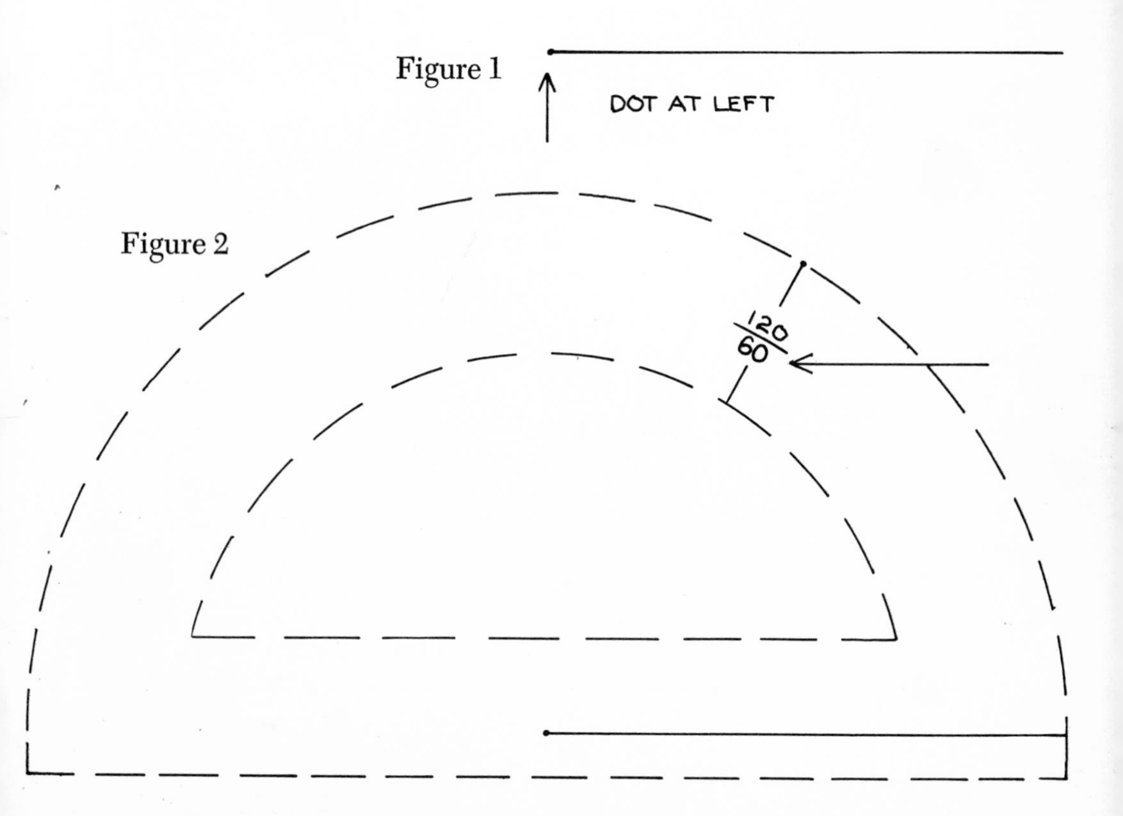

Figure 1

Figure 2

3. Connect the dots so that your new line is also 3 inches long. See the broken line in the drawing.

4. Using the *new* line (the broken one in Figure 3) and the dot at the left, mark another 60-degree angle. Notice that the dot at the left in Figure 3 is still the dot at the left on your new line.

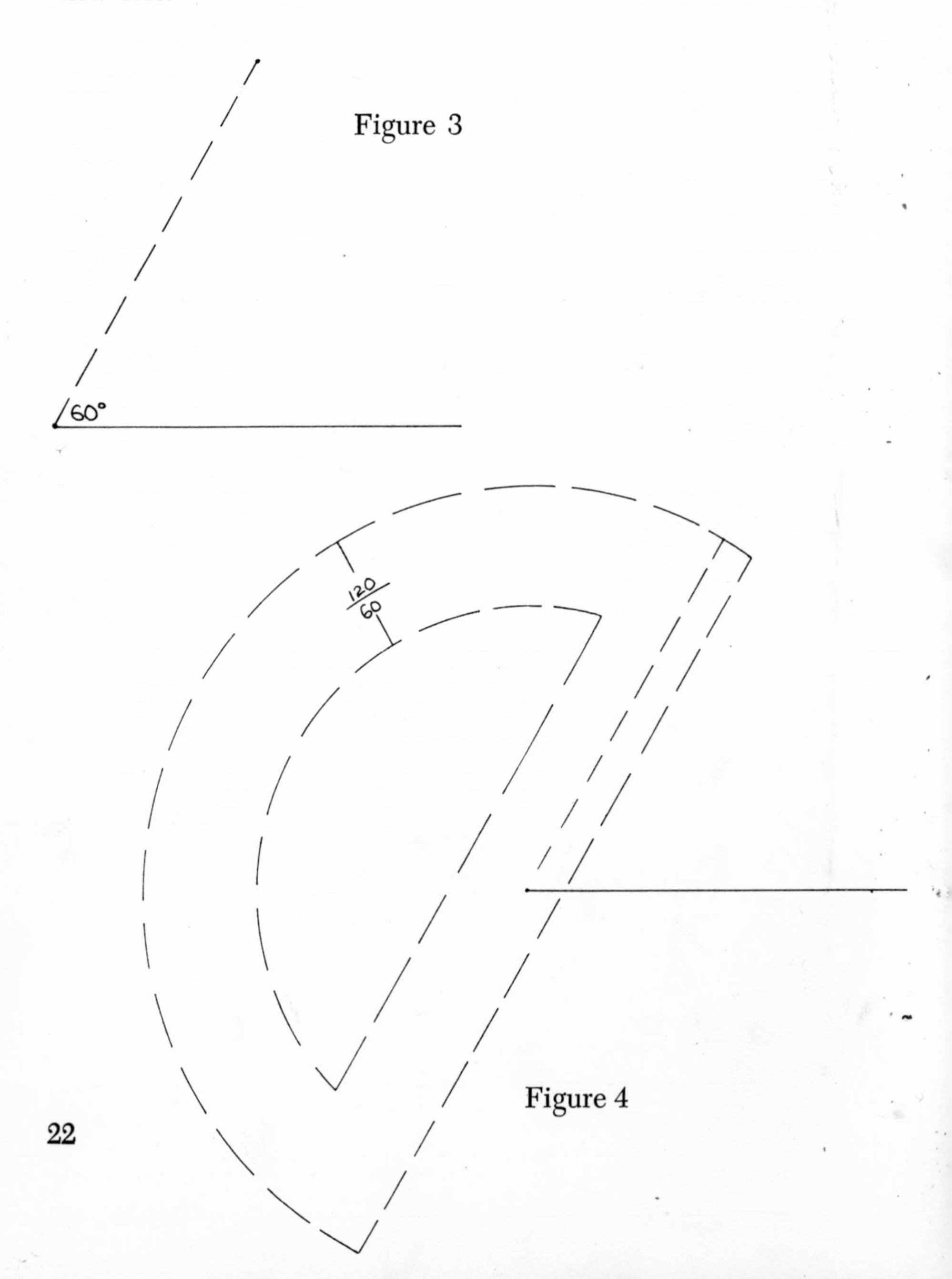

Figure 3

Figure 4

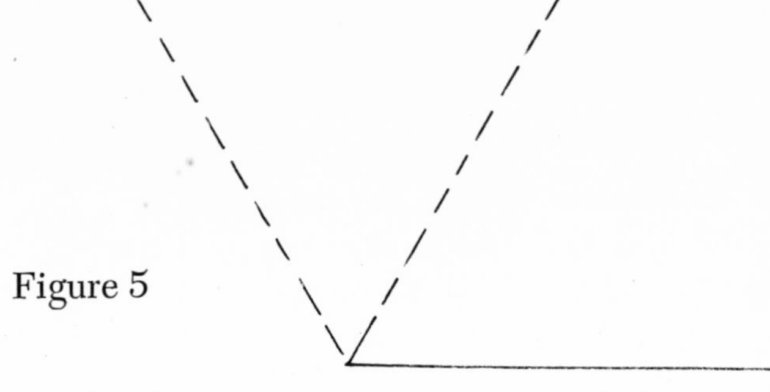

Figure 5

5. Connect the dots with another new 3-inch line.
6. Continue making 60-degree angles until you have six lines coming out like spokes from the center of a wheel. Remember to measure from the *new* line and the dot on the left each time.
7. Connect the outer points of the six lines. You have a perfect hexagon—if you worked accurately. In Figure 6 the broken line forms the hexagon.

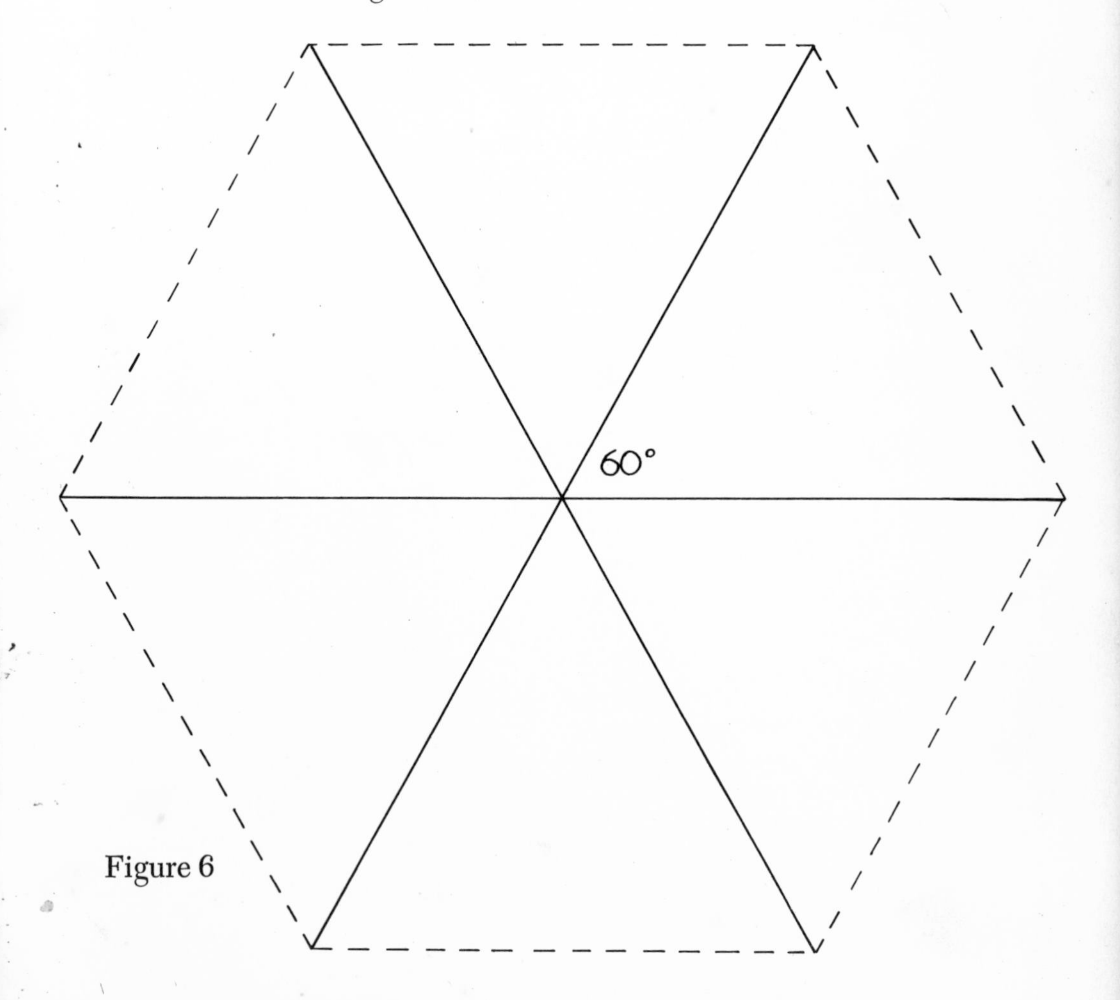

Figure 6

Making an Octagon

An octagon is as easy to make as a hexagon. The difference is at the center, where you'll use 45-degree angles instead of 60-degree angles. Since there are eight 45's in 360, you will have eight equal 45-degree angles and eight equal straight sides—an octagon.

1. Draw a 3-inch line and put a dot at the left end.

2. Use your protractor and mark a 45-degree angle, remembering that when the dot is at the left, you use the numerals under the curved line.

3. Connect the dots so that your new line is also 3 inches long.

4. Measuring from the *new* line and the dot at the left mark another 45-degree angle; connect the dots for another new 3-inch line.

Figure 1

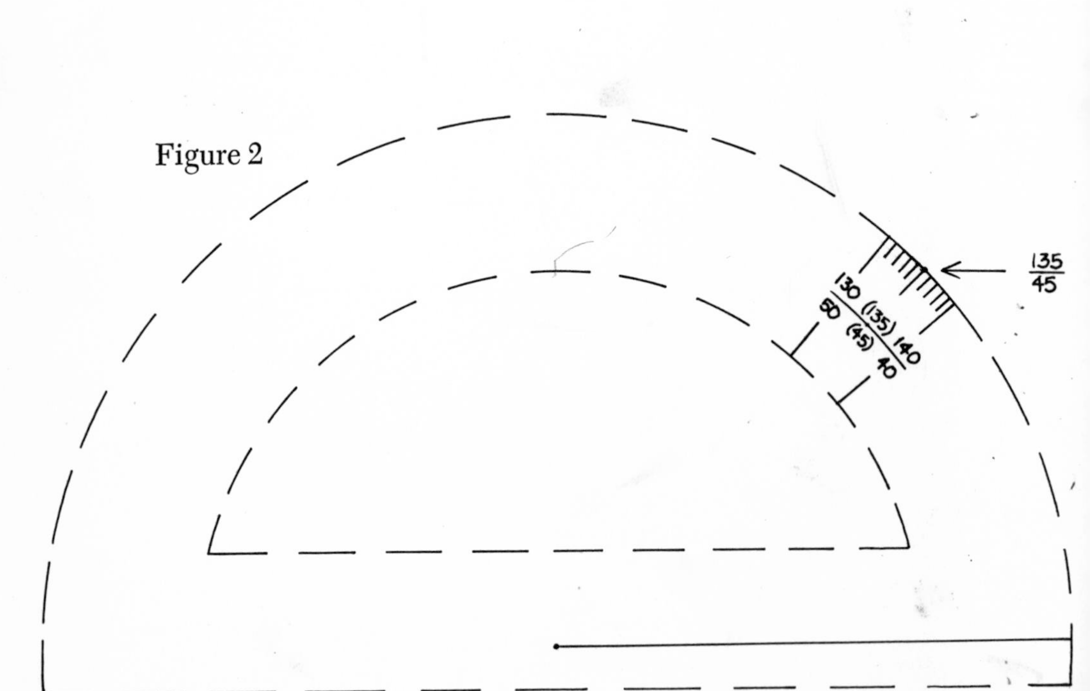

Figure 2

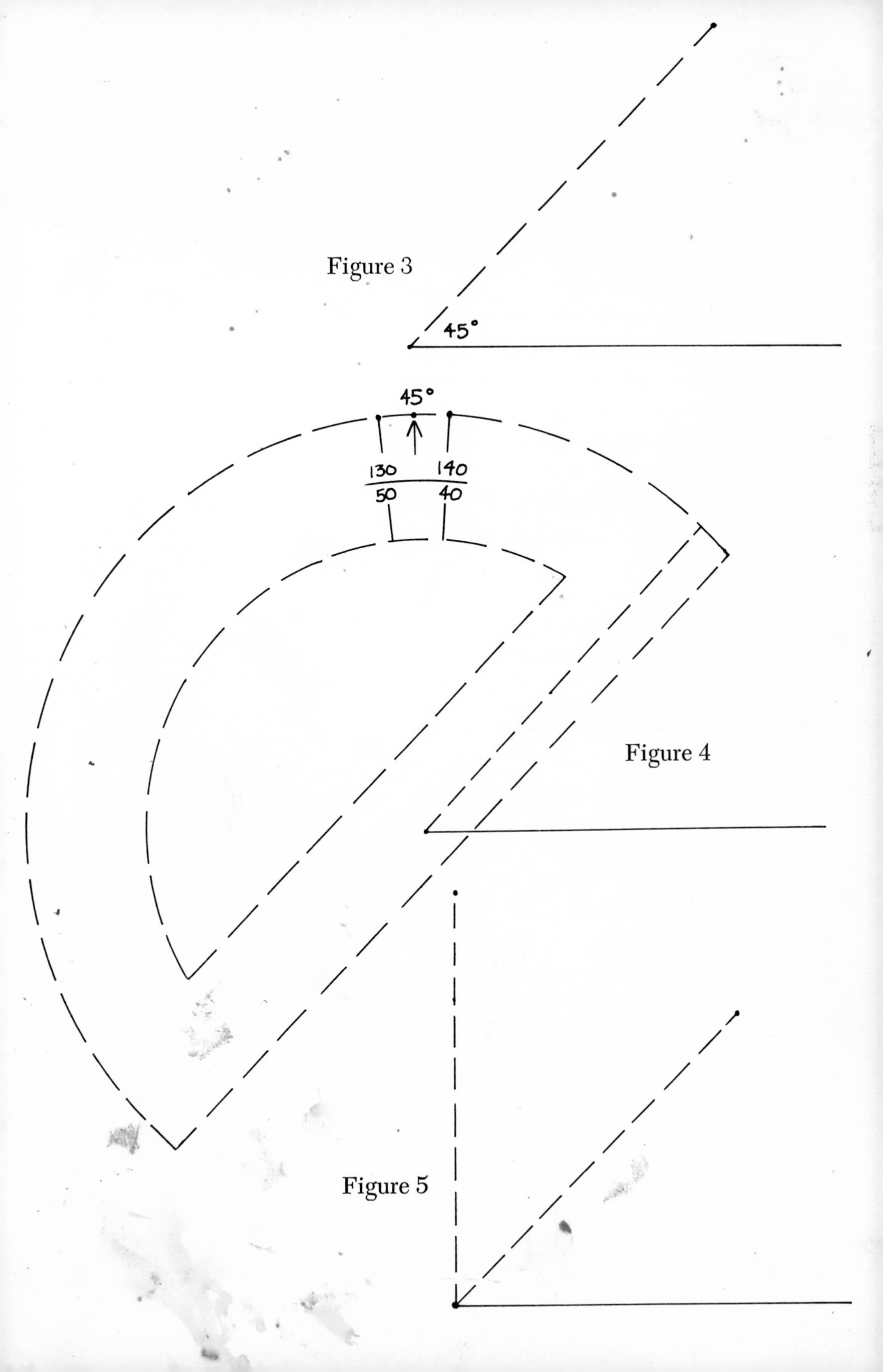
Figure 3
45°
45°
130
50
140
40
Figure 4
Figure 5

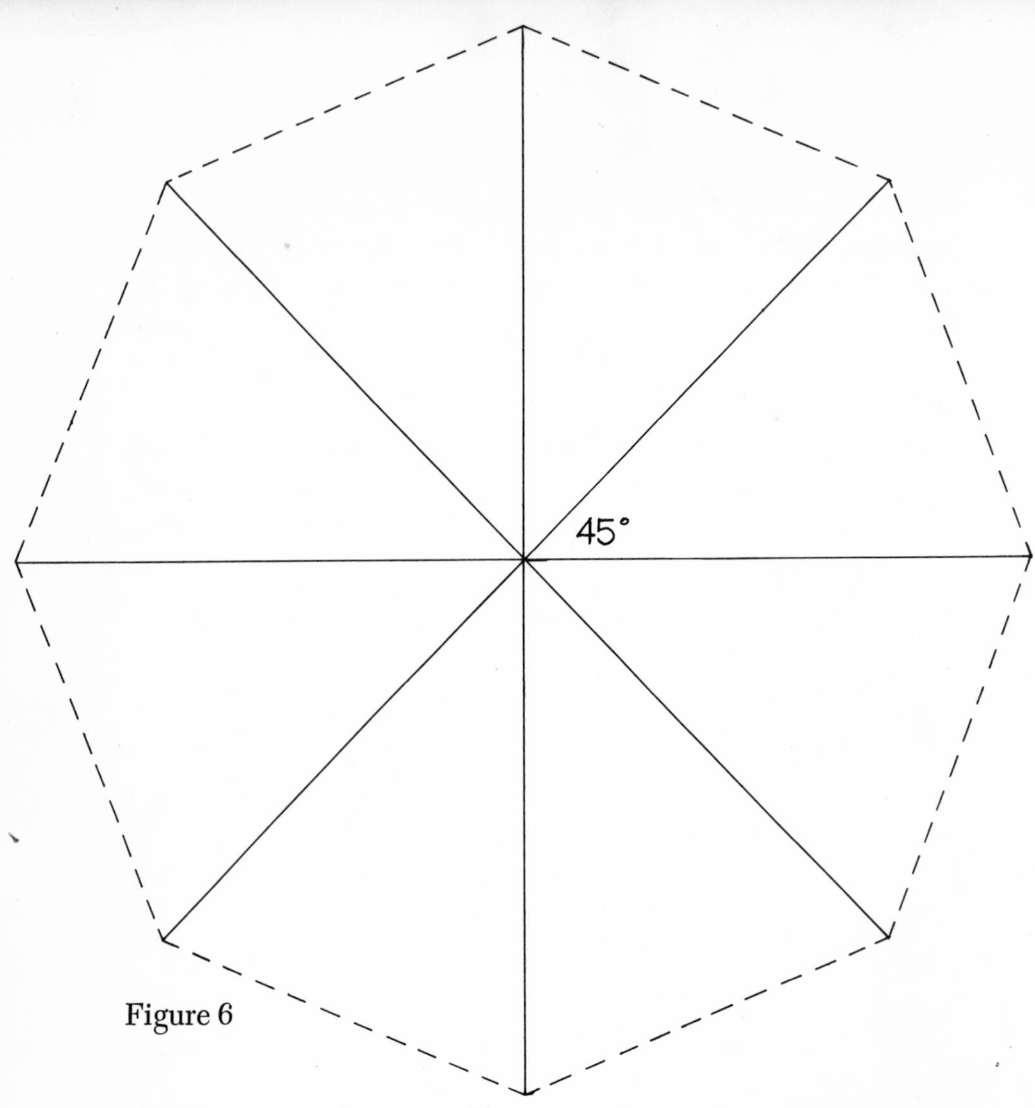

Figure 6

5. Continue making 45 degree angles until you have eight lines coming out like spokes from the center of a wheel. Use the new line and the dot to the left each time.
6. Connect the outer points of your eight lines. You now have a perfect eight-sided figure—an octagon. The broken line in Figure 6 forms the octagon.

Making a Pentagon
If you use 72-degree angles at the center, you will have a five-sided figure—a pentagon. Start with a 3-inch line; but if you want a larger figure, start with a longer line. Each new line

you make must be as long as the one you started with. Otherwise, you couldn't get a perfect figure. If you want a small pentagon, start with a 1- or 2-inch line. Keep all your new lines the same length as the first one. After you have all of the spokes in, connect the outer points to complete your figure.

Making Other Polygons

Thirty-six-degree angles at the center will give you a ten-sided figure. Can you figure out the angle size for a twelve-sided figure? If you can divide 360 degrees into twelve equal parts, you can!

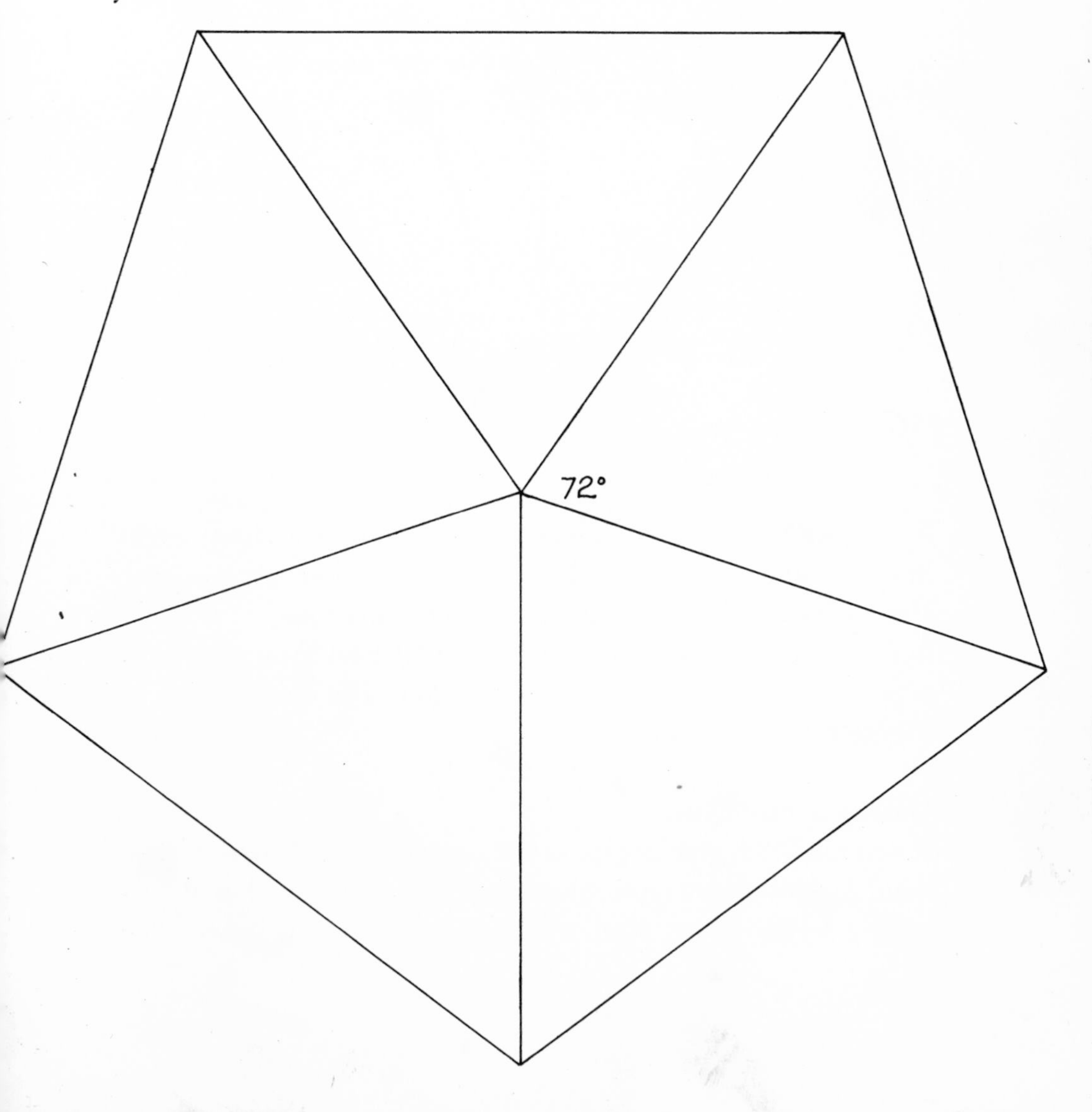

Five-Pointed Stars

Here's an easy way to make a perfect five-pointed star.

1. Use 72-degree angles at the center, and draw 3-inch lines. There will be five, since there are five 72's in 360.

2. When you have the five spokes, don't connect the outer points as you did when making the pentagon. Instead, using your ruler, extend one 3-inch spoke through the dot so that the line goes between the two opposite 3-inch lines, as shown in Figure 2. Your extended line may be from 1 to 1½ inches long.

3. Extend each of the other spokes the same way, keeping all of the extended lines the same length.

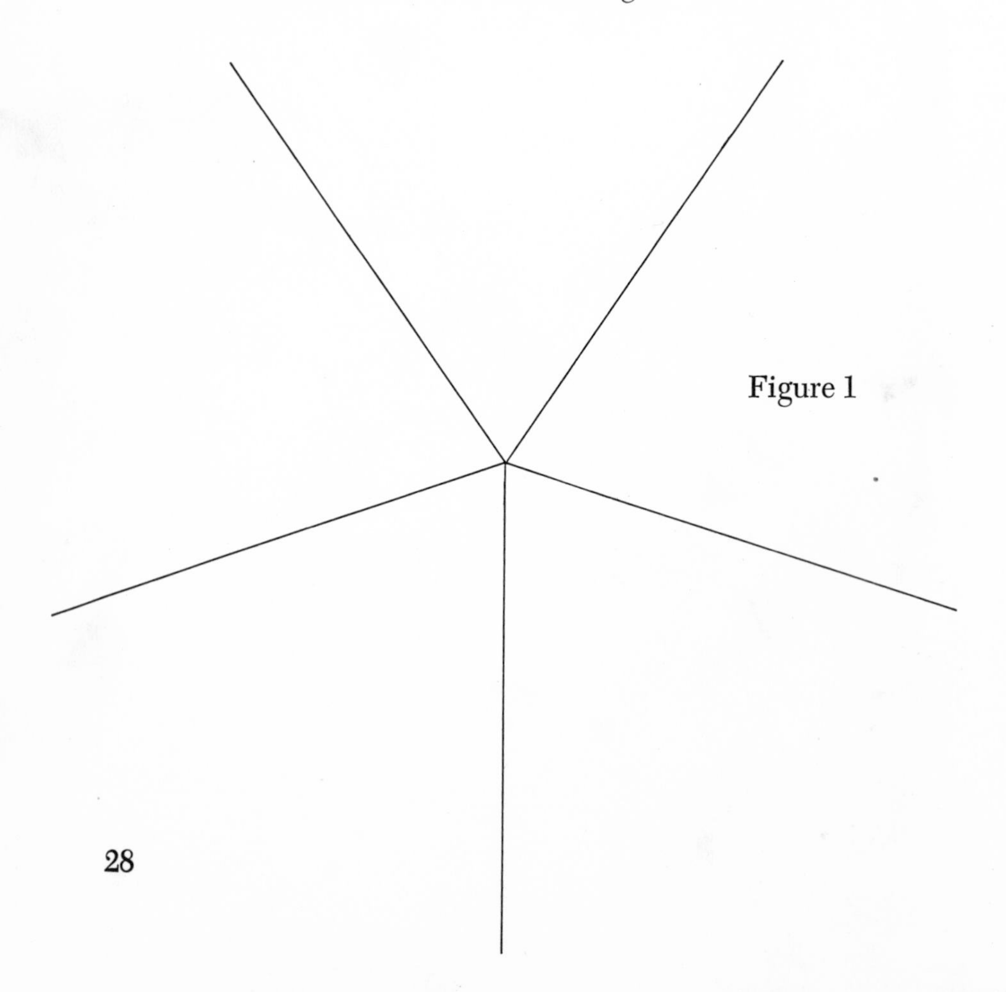

Figure 1

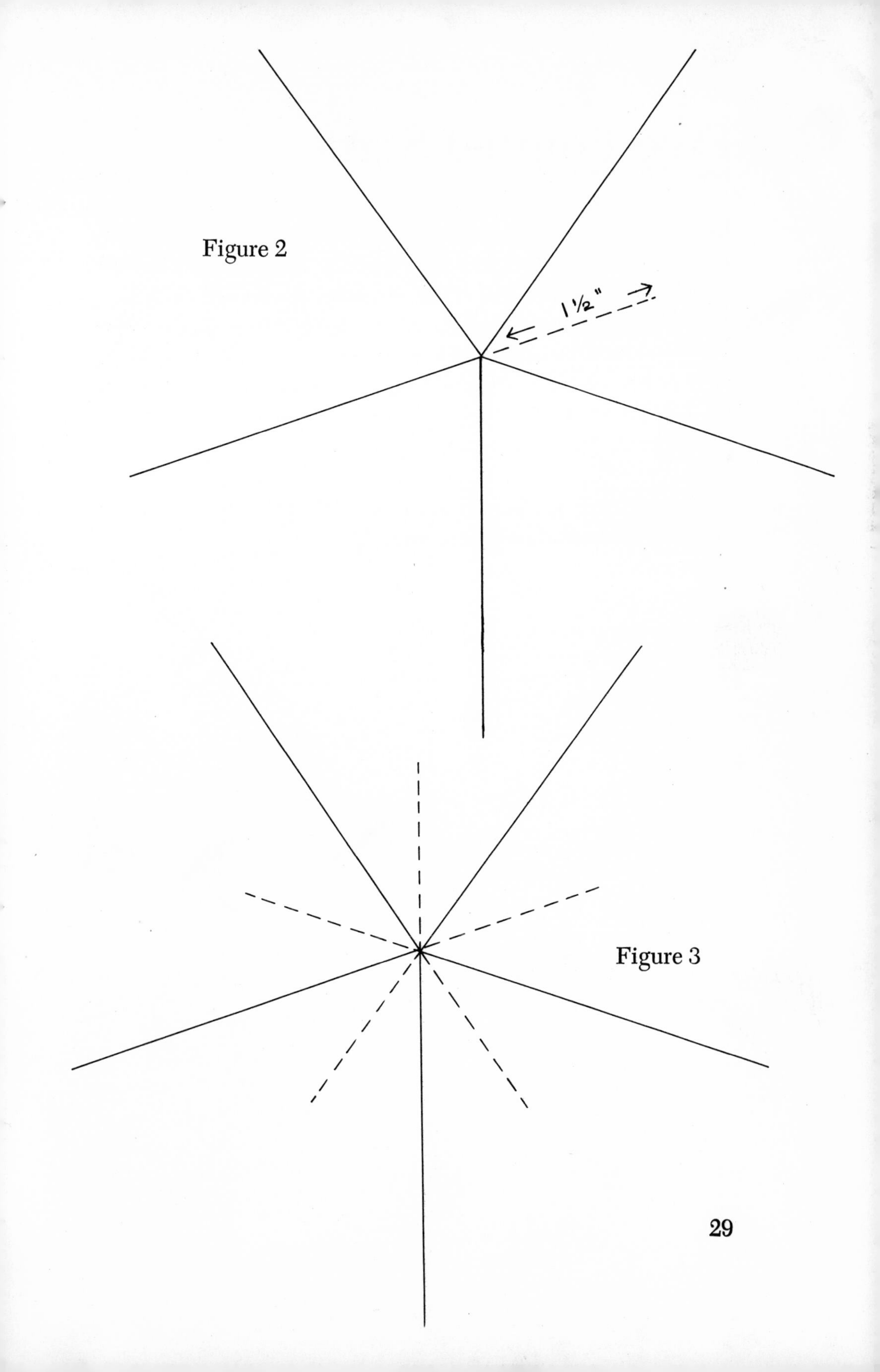

Figure 2
1½"
Figure 3

4. Connect the outer points of all the lines, and you have a perfect five-pointed star.

Make several stars, using different lengths for the extended parts while keeping the first five spokes 3 inches long. Notice that the shorter your extended lines are, the sharper your star points will be. In Figure 5 the extended lines are 1-inch long.

If you like "fat stars," make your extended lines longer. They are 2 inches long in Figure 6.

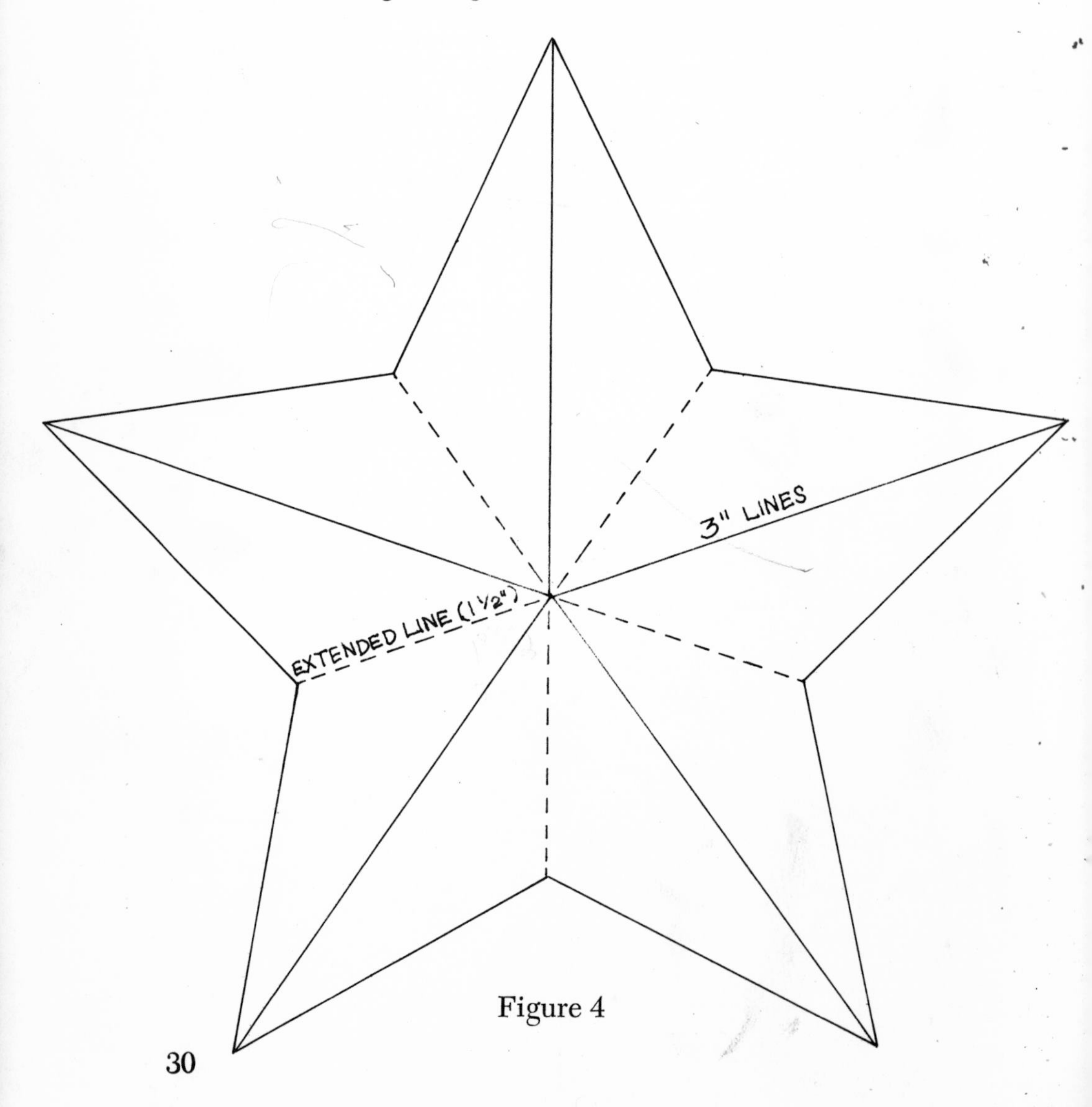

Figure 4

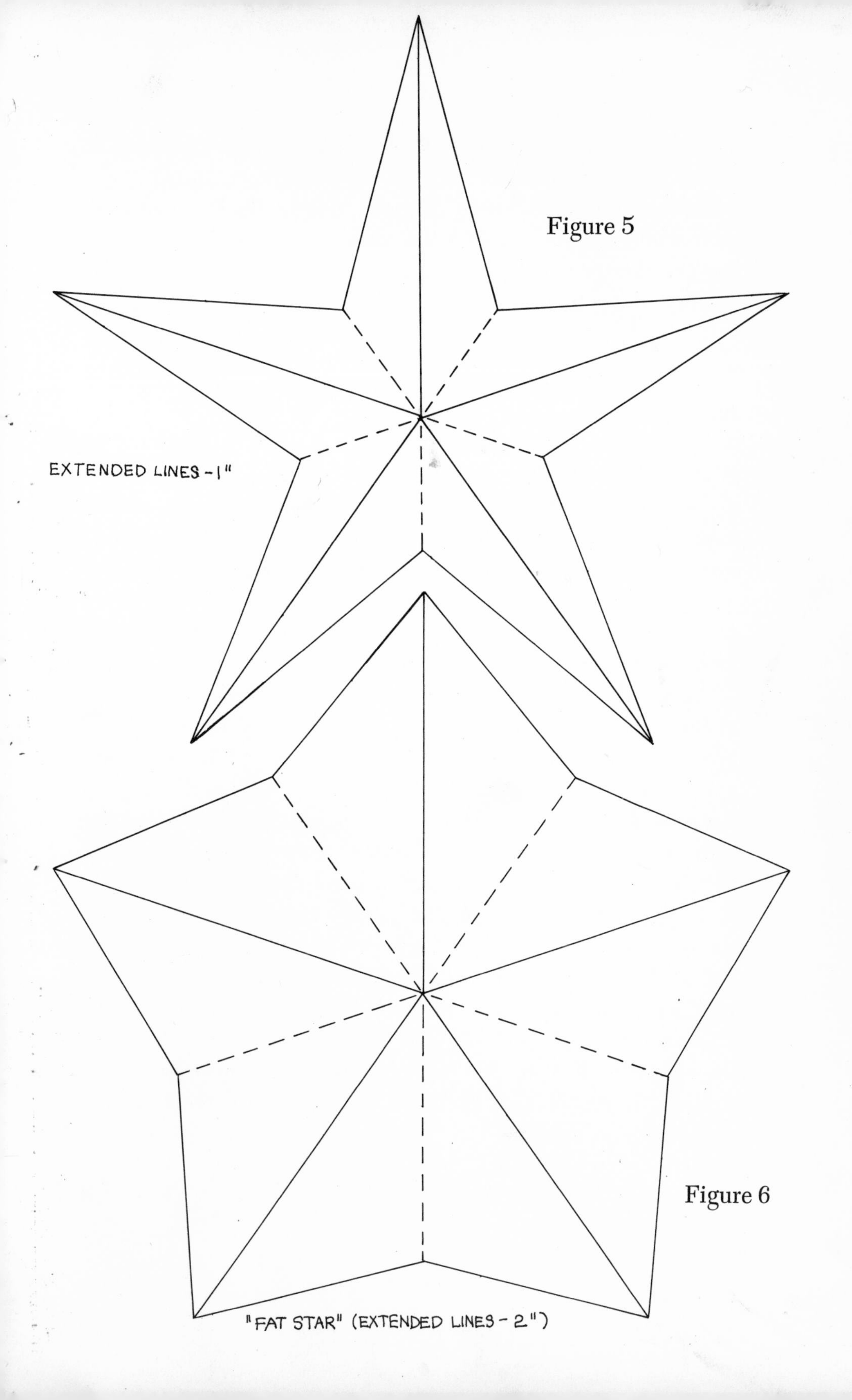

Figure 5

Figure 6

From Straight Lines to Curves

Do you know you can make a curved line by using only straight lines? Use a sharp pencil. Remember: just *one* step at a time.

1. Make a 90-degree angle, with each line exactly 3-inches long.

2. Using your ruler, put a dot at each ¼-inch marking on both lines. Hold your pencil straight up and twist it to get accurate markings. Count the dots on each line; you should have thirteen. The dot where the angle is formed (vertex) has to be counted twice, once for each line. Though you counted this dot twice, it's the only one you won't be using when you start making your curve. Your drawing so far should look like Figure 1.

3. Letter the drawing, following Figure 2. Start with an A at the right end of the base line, and letter toward the vertex. You will letter just twelve dots, since you won't be using the vertex. Did you end with the letter L?

Letter the vertical line from A through L, but this time start with the dot just above the vertex. Your design looks like Figure 2 if you followed directions carefully.

4. In this step you will need to be very accurate in connecting the dots. Connect the dots marked A. Look very carefully at Figure 3. Now connect the dots marked B. Be sure you connect the right dots! Go on to the C's, the D's, and so on, until you have finished with the L's. Notice that you did not use the vertex at all. Your design should look like Figure 4.

Hold the design away from you. See the curved line that was made with straight lines?

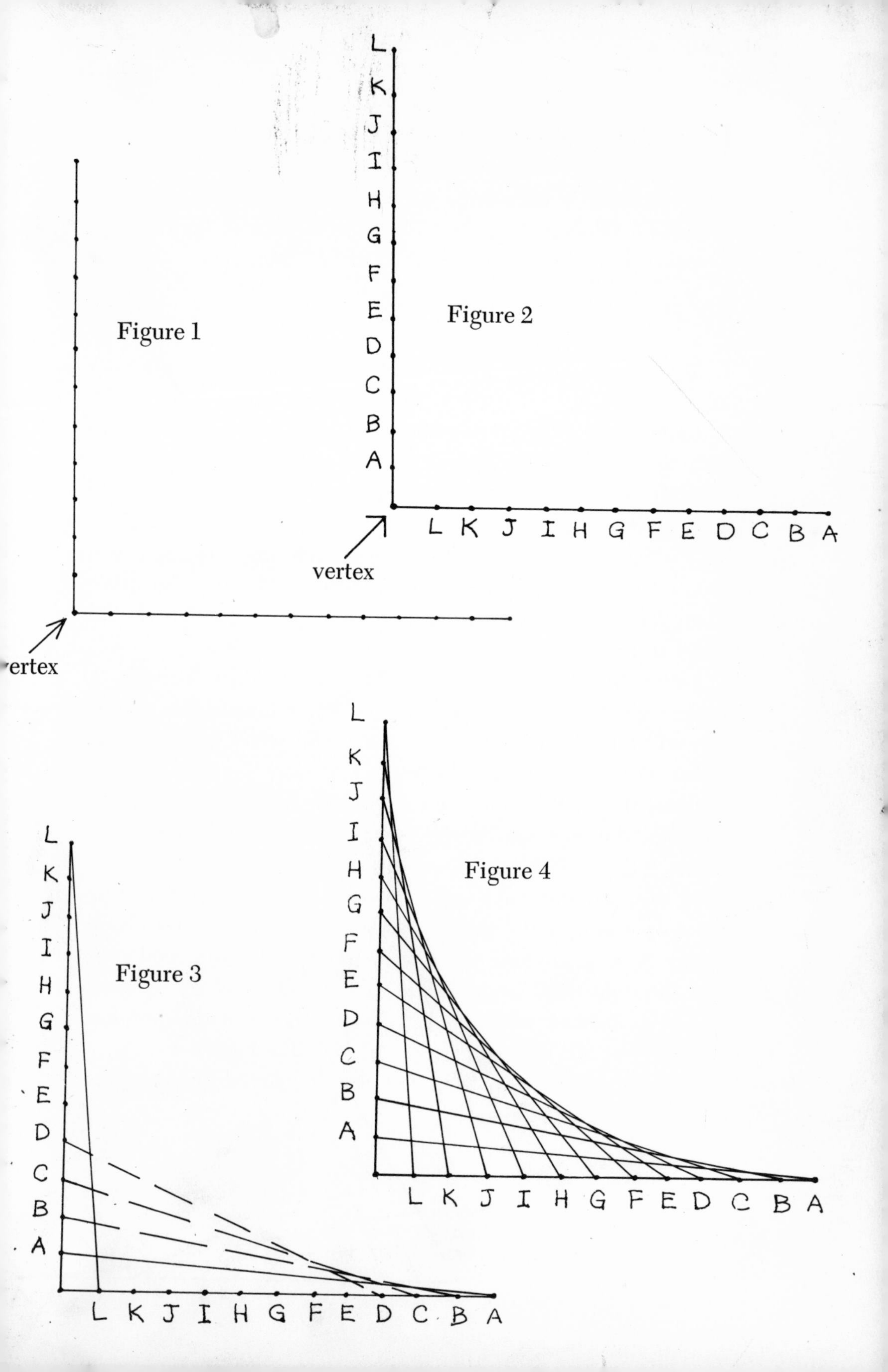
Figure 1
vertex
Figure 2
L K J I H G F E D C B A
L K J I H G F E D C B A
vertex
Figure 3
L K J I H G F E D C B A
L K J I H G F E D C B A
Figure 4
L K J I H G F E D C B A
L K J I H G F E D C B A

Trying Different Angles to Get Different Curves

Each time you change the size of the angle, you will get a different curve. This design uses a 60-degree angle.

1. Make a 60-degree angle. Check pages 21 and 22 if you've forgotten how. Keep your lines 3-inches long.

2. Mark the lines exactly as you did your 90-degree angle, dots ¼-inch apart and letters from A through L on both lines. Don't letter the corner dot, or vertex.

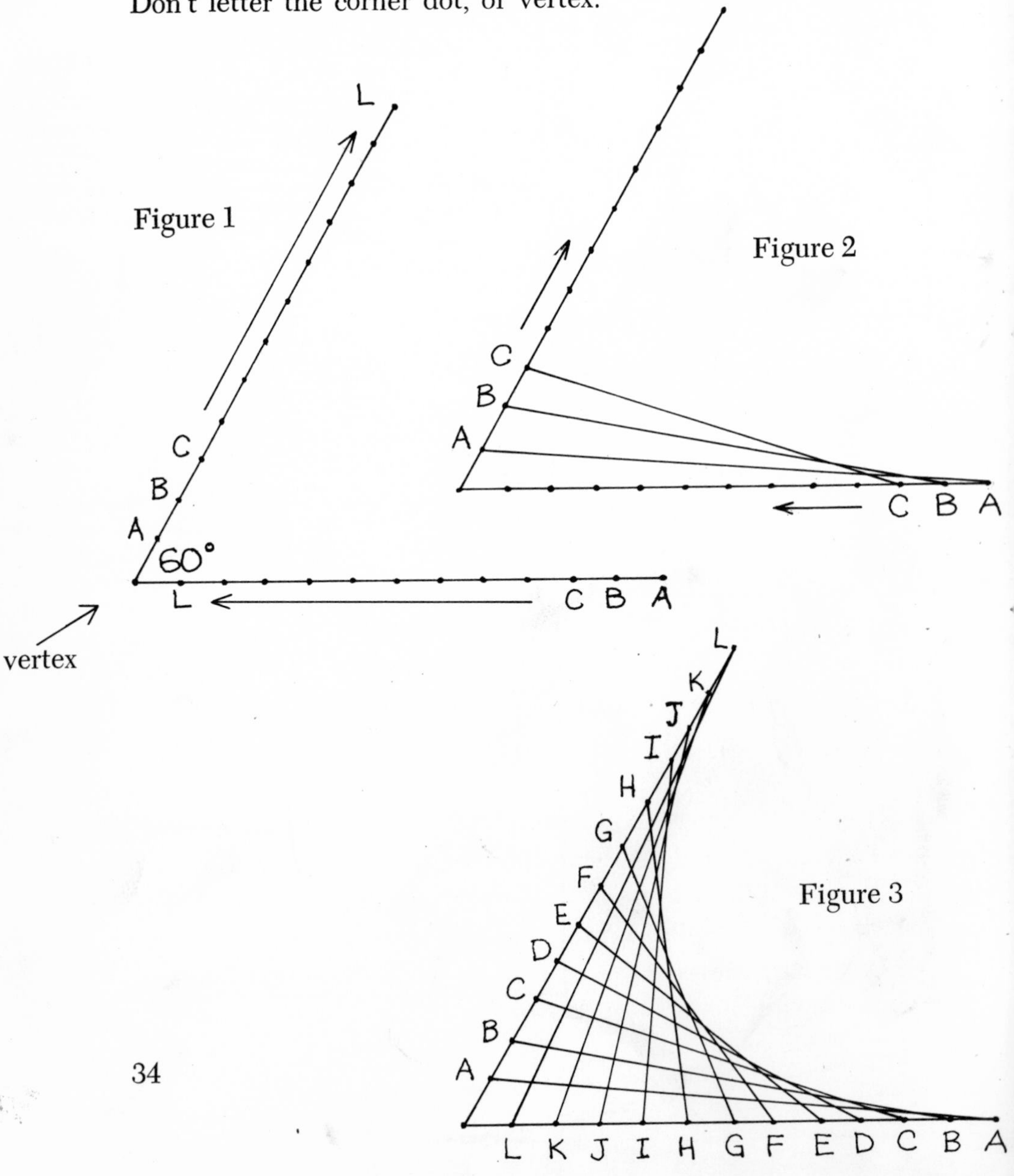

Figure 1

Figure 2

Figure 3

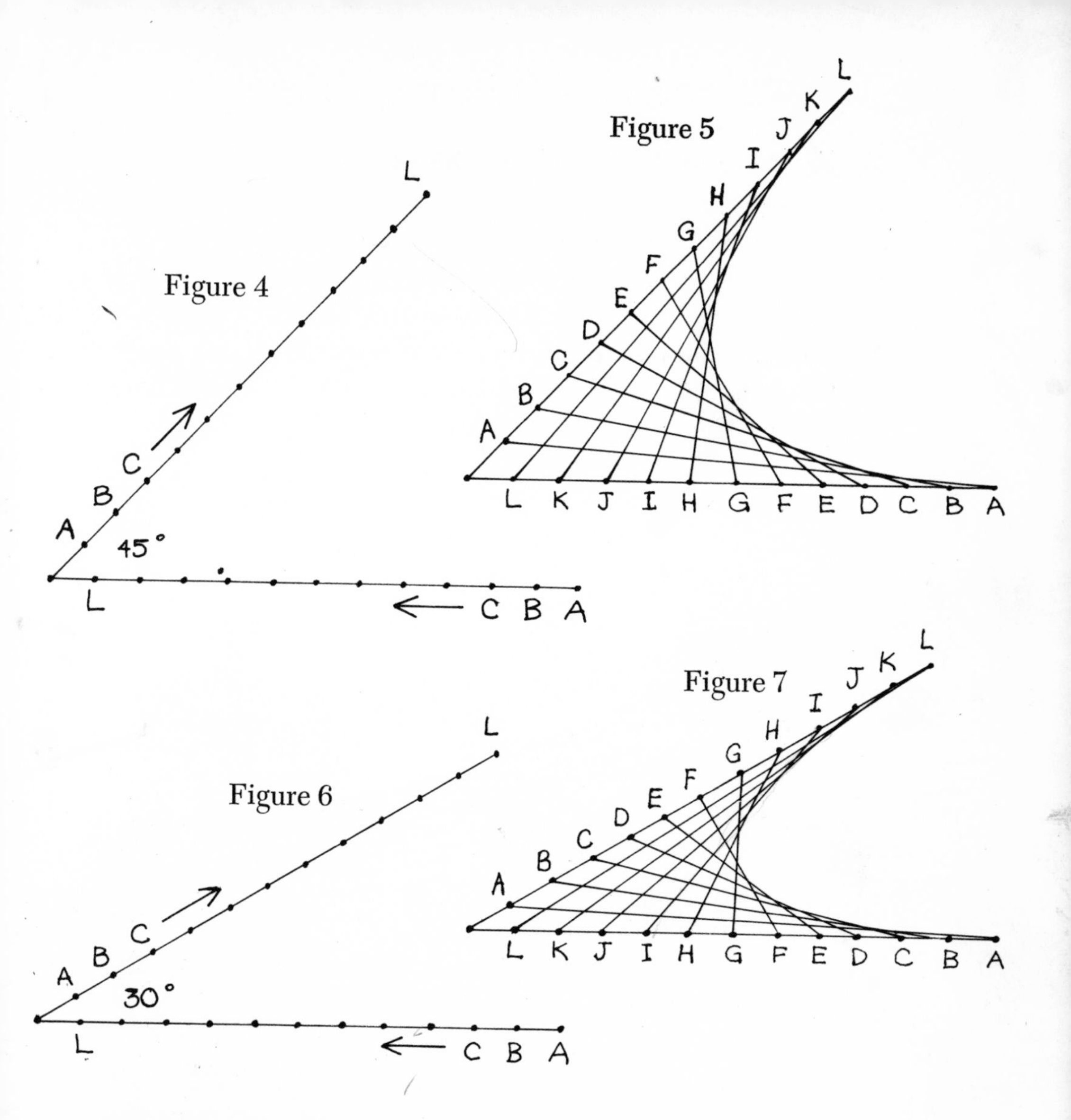

3. Connect your A's, your B's, your C's, and so on, through the L's, just as you did before. Your design should look like Figure 3.

Hold your completed designs (90 and 60 degree angles) away from you and see how different the curves are.

To make a drawing using a 45-degree angle, start it as shown in Figure 4. Complete it as shown in Figure 5.

Using a 30-degree angle, start as shown in Figure 6. Complete your drawing as shown in Figure 7.

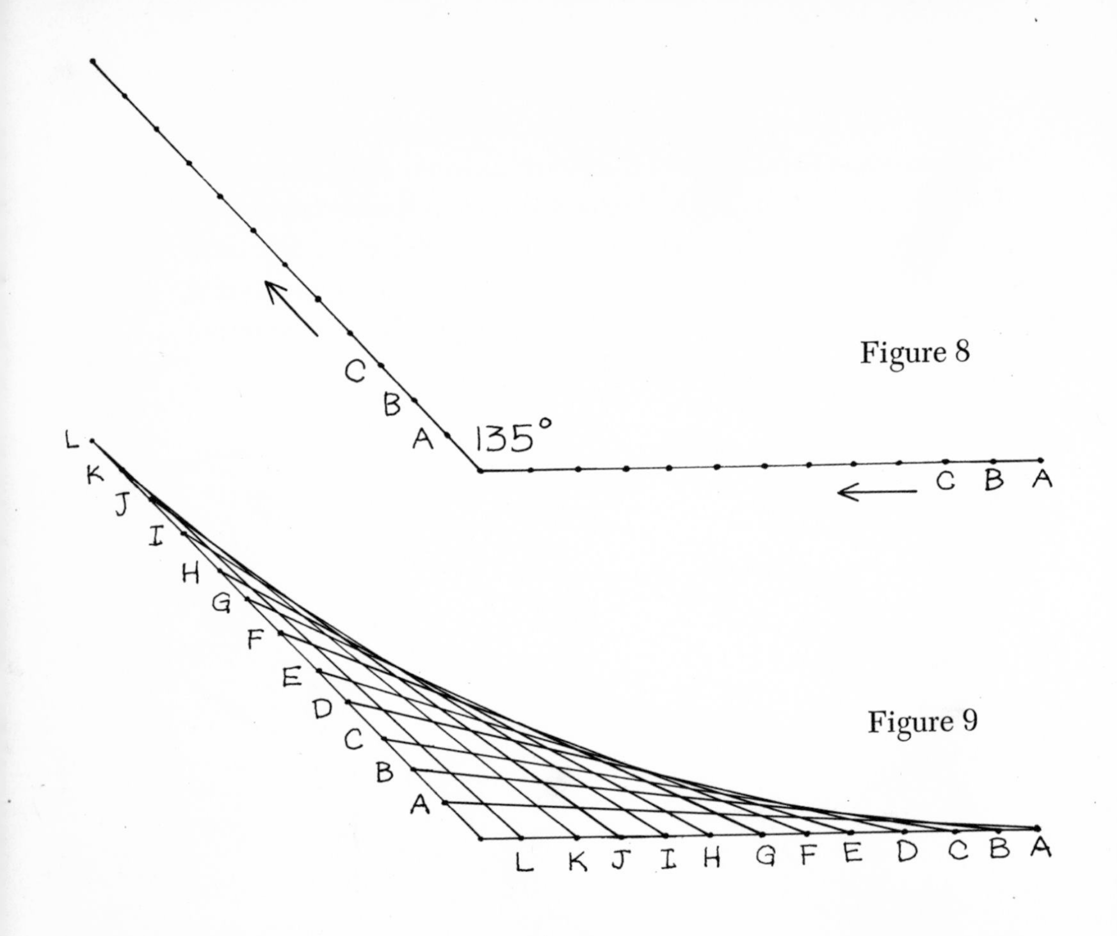

When making a 135-degree angle, remember to keep the lines of your angle the same length. Start as shown in Figure 8. Complete your drawing as shown in Figure 9.

Notice that the lettering is the same no matter what the size of the angle. Remember, always letter one line from the farthest point toward the vertex. Letter the other line by starting one dot above the vertex and working away from it. Be sure that you have the same number of dots on each line and that the dots are ¼-inch apart.

After you have carefully made a drawing from each of the different angles, line them up by sizes, putting the smallest first and the largest last. Notice that the larger the angle is. the closer the curve gets to a straight line.

After you have completed many drawings, you may find that you won't need to letter your dots anymore. Just remember that you always start at the farthest dot from the vertex on one line. Start one dot up from the vertex on the other line and work toward the end of the line. Always keep the same number of dots on each line. If you get confused, go back to lettering the dots for a while.

Designs From Squares

You can make all kinds of designs now that you know what kind of curve each angle will give.

1. Draw a 4-inch square. You can make a perfect one now because you know that a square has four right, or 90-degree, angles, and with your protractor you can easily make 90-degree angles.

2. Put dots ¼-inch apart on each line (see Figure 1).

3. Using the bottom line of the square and the one on the left, make a curve, as you did with your 90-degree angle on page 33.

Figure 1

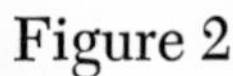
Figure 2

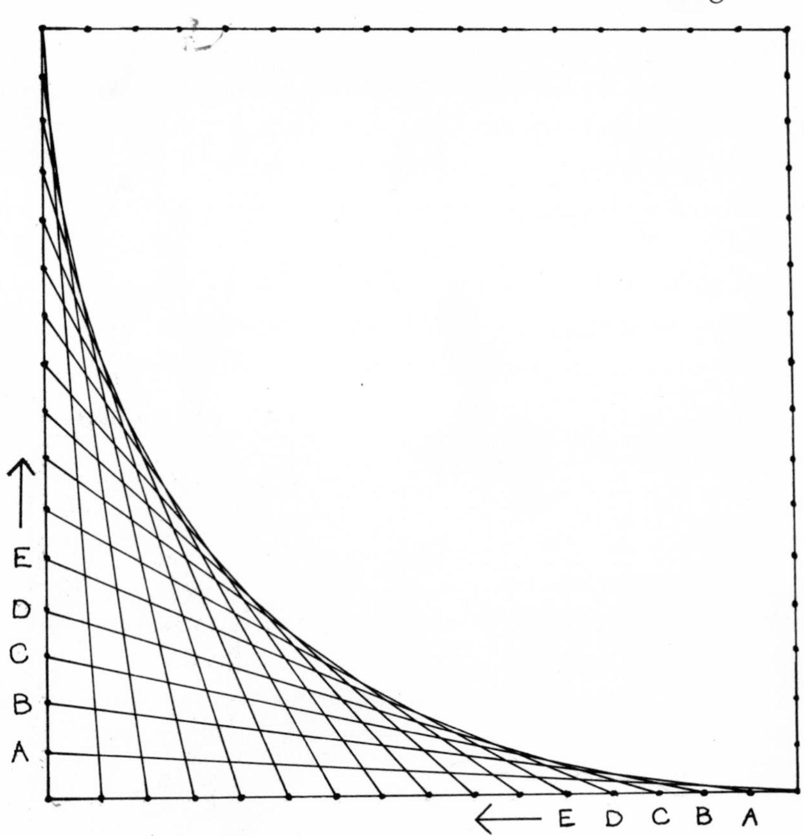

4. Use the top line and the one on the right. Work this design just the opposite of the one you just finished. That is, start at the far left of your top line (see Figure 3 on the next page) and work toward the right. On the right-side line, start with the dot under the vertex (A^1 in Figure 3) and work *down.* Connect A and A^1 with a straight line. Then connect B with B^1, C with C^1, and so on. If you prefer, you may turn your design upside down and work the design as you did in what is now the lower left angle.

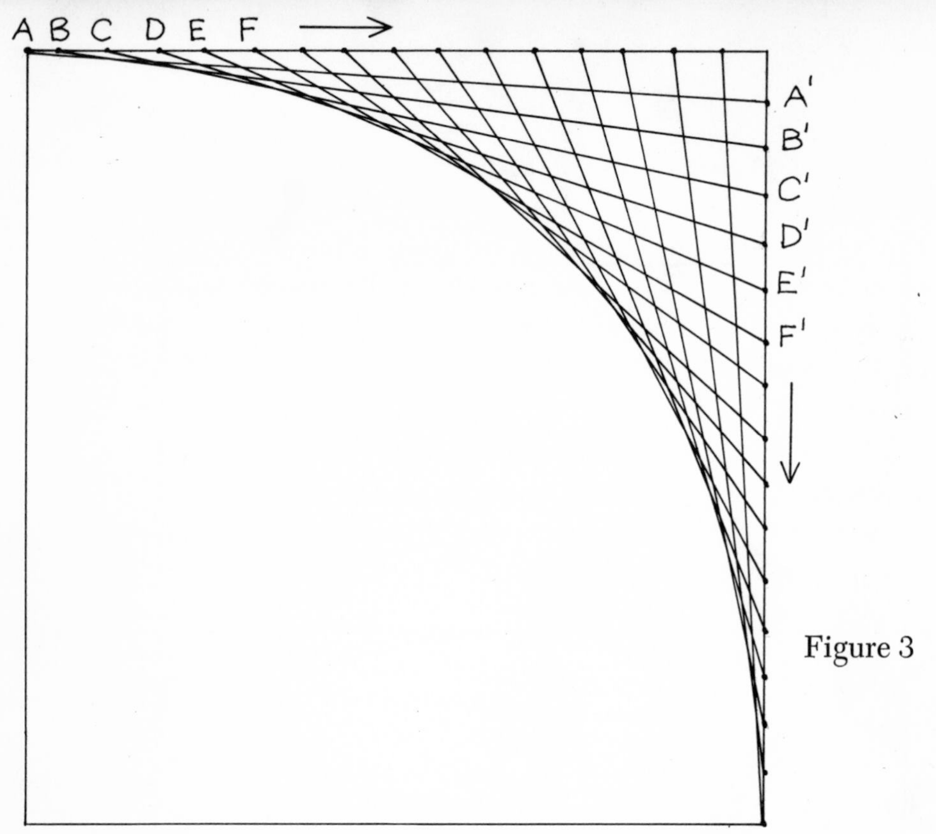

Figure 3

When your design is finished, you will have an open space that looks like an eye.

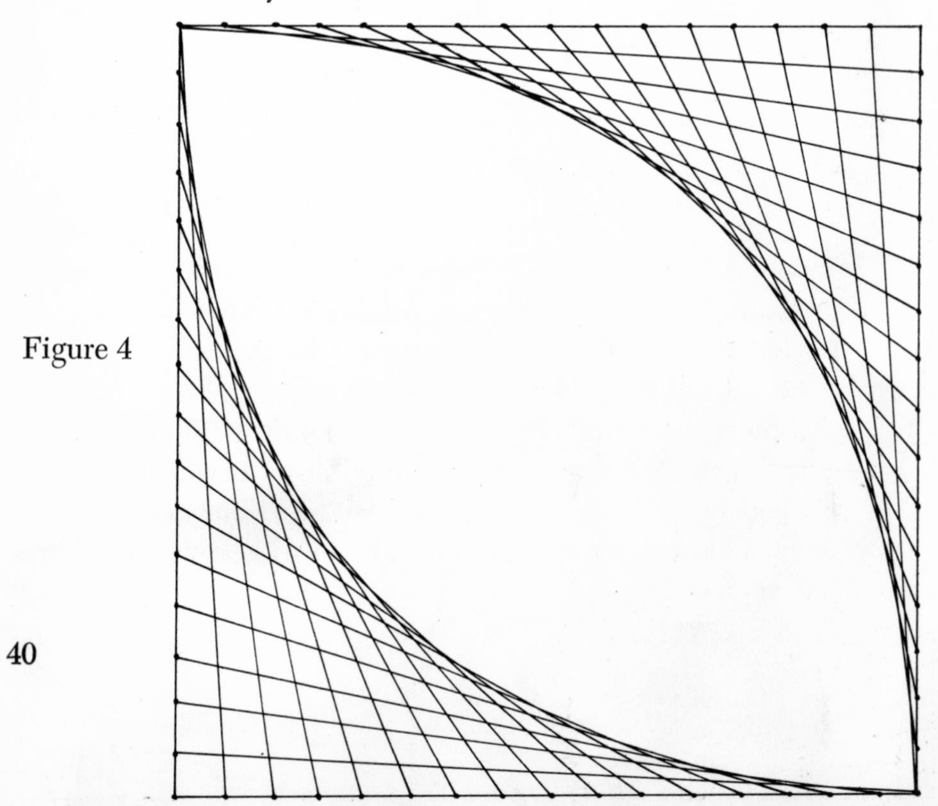
Figure 4

You can work from any corner of your square. Sometimes lines will overlap, but this will help make different designs.

The next five designs are made by using different combinations of two designs you have already made: the 90-degree-angle curve on page 33 and the finished design (Figure 4) on page 40.

Design 1

The first design has four 4-inch squares that use the design on page 40. The "eyes" are there, going around in a circle.

1. Make an 8-inch square. (Remember, all angles are 90-degree angles in a square.)

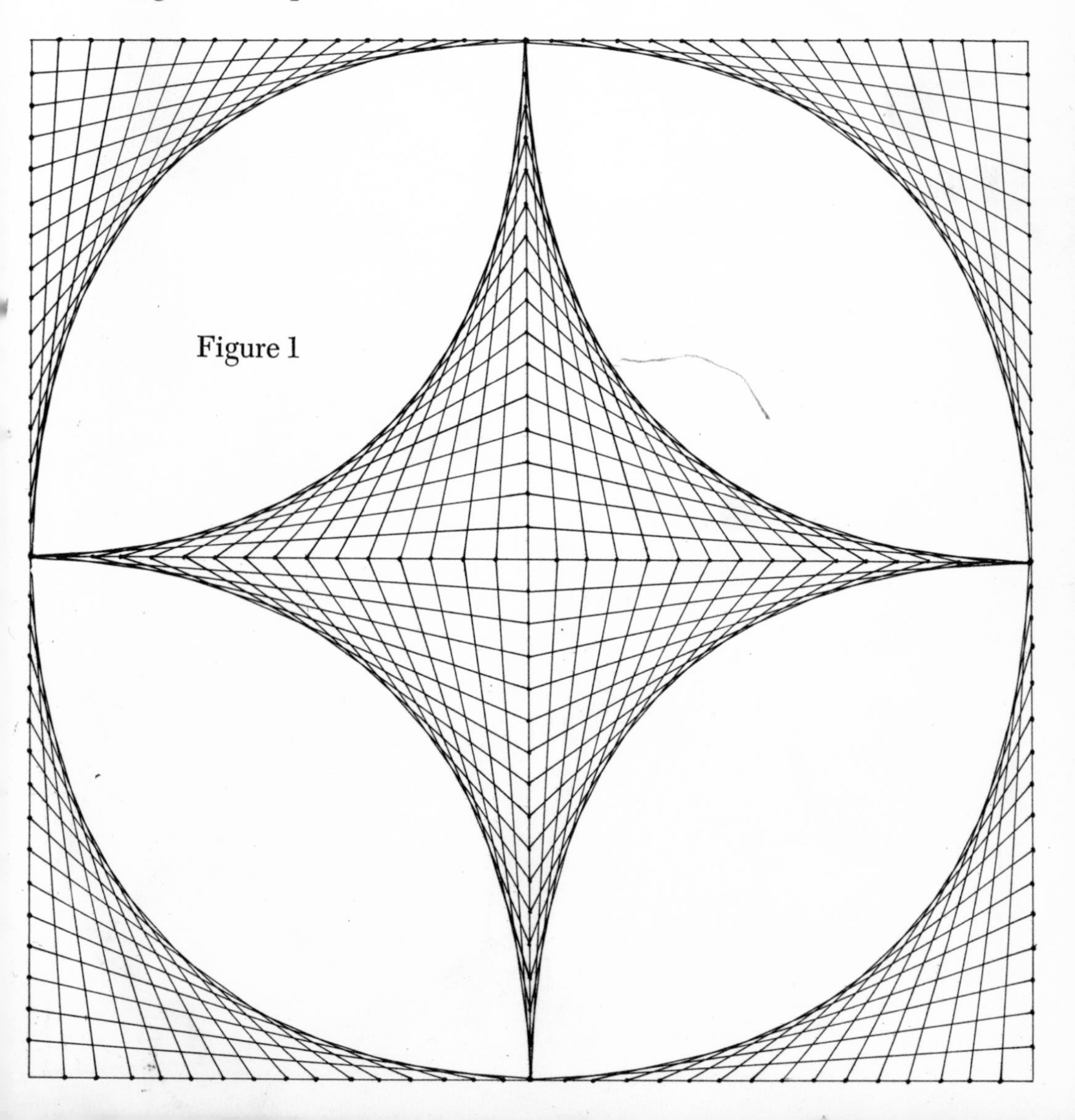

Figure 1

2. Using your ruler again, find the halfway point on each 8-inch line. (It will be 4 inches from the corner.)

3. Connect the dots on opposite lines. You now have four 4-inch squares adjoining each other. Mark dots ¼-inch apart on all of your lines.

4. Work with one square at a time, making the same design you did in Figure 4 on page 40. Start with the square at the lower left.

5. Turn your paper so that the finished part of your design is

Figure 2

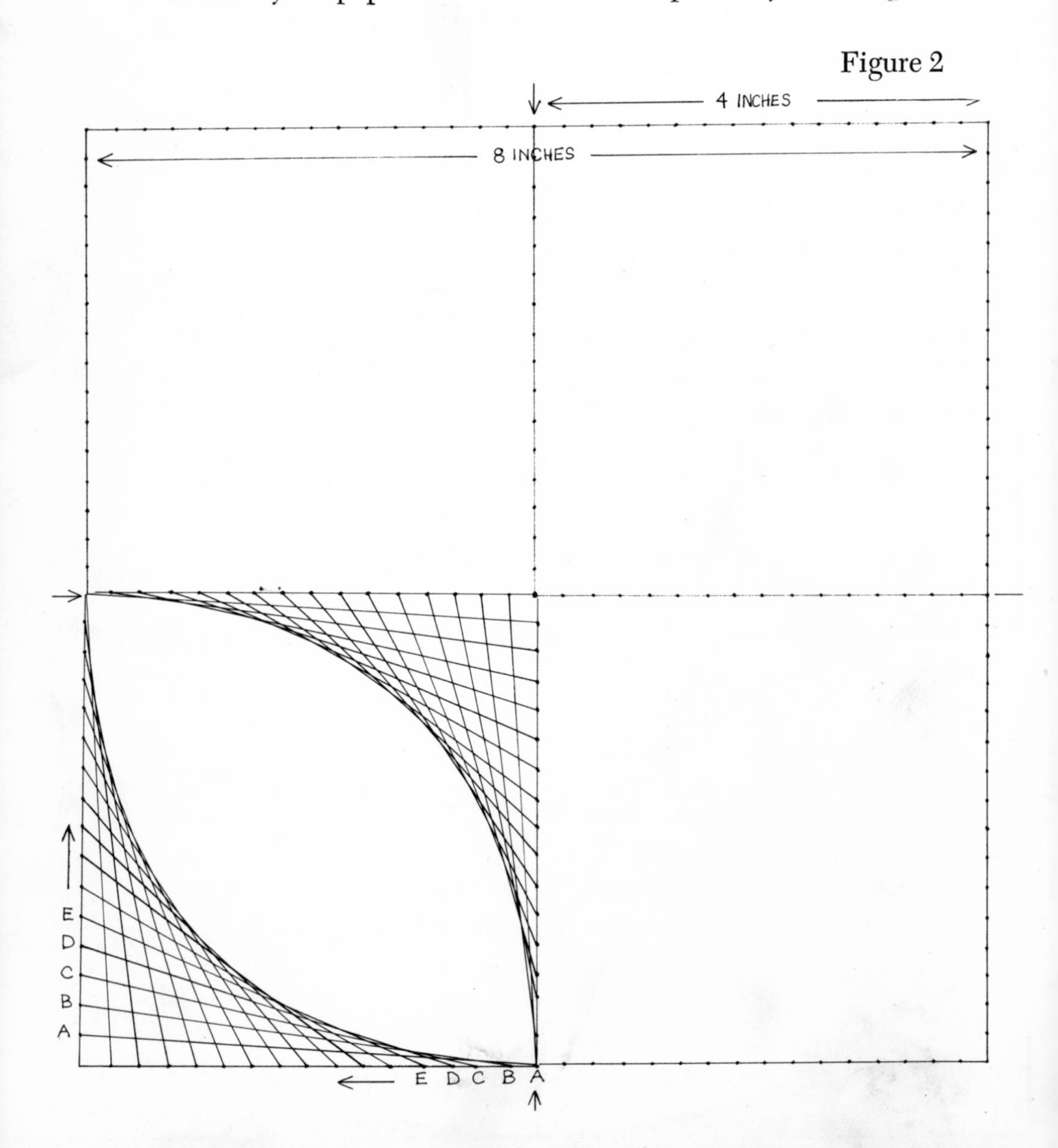

FINISHED DESIGN

WORK THIS DESIGN; TURN PAPER ONCE AGAIN, AND WORK LAST DESIGN.

FINISHED DESIGN

Figure 3

at the lower right, and work the new lower-left square exactly as you did the first one.

6. Continue moving the paper around the same way, each time working the lower-left corner until all four squares are finished.

Design 2

1. Make your 8-inch square. (See Steps 1 to 3 in Design 1.)

2. Work only the angles that are marked with an x in Figure 1. The dotted line shows you where the curved line will be in each of the four squares.

3. The completed design is shown in Figure 2.

Figure 1

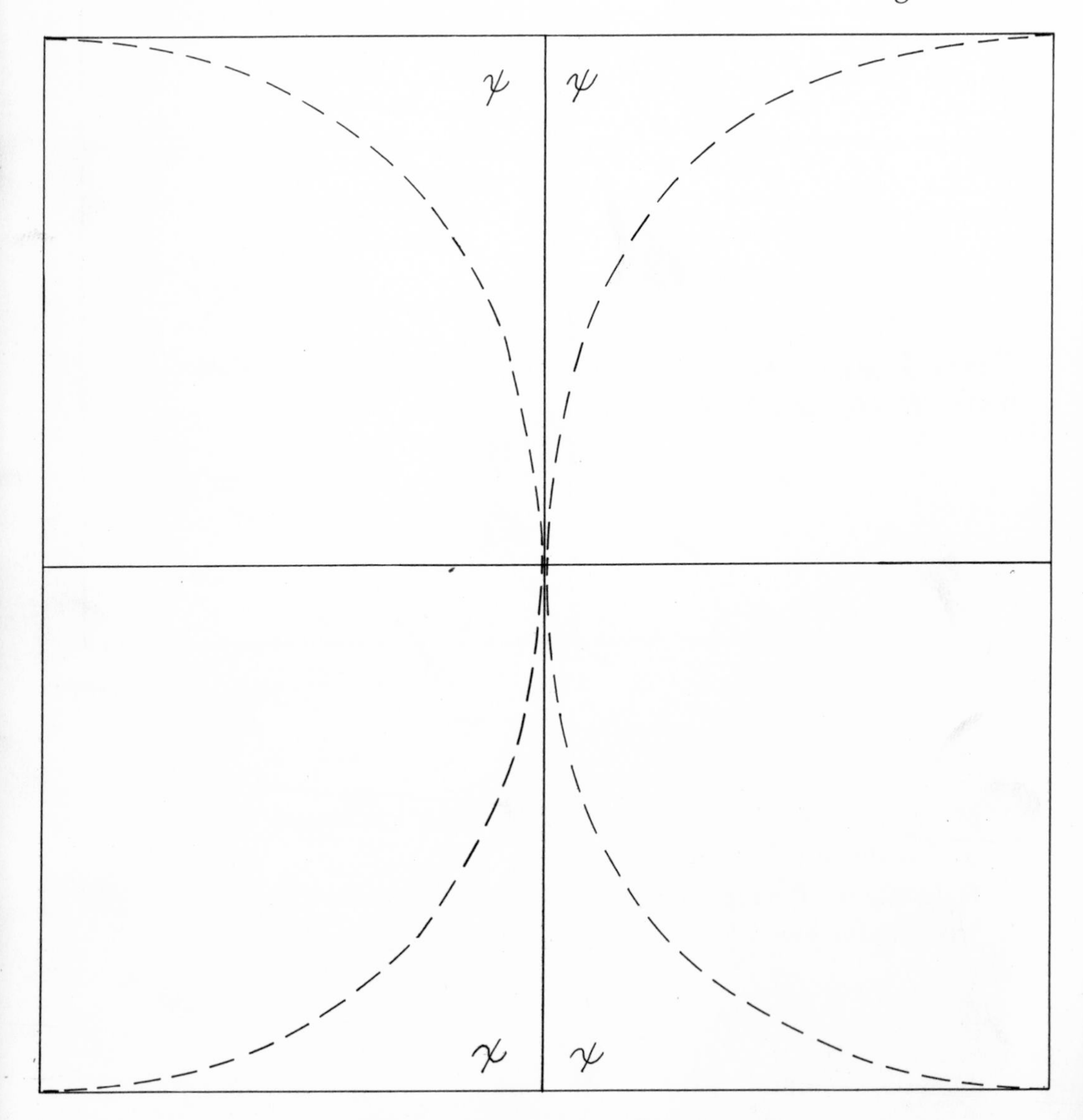

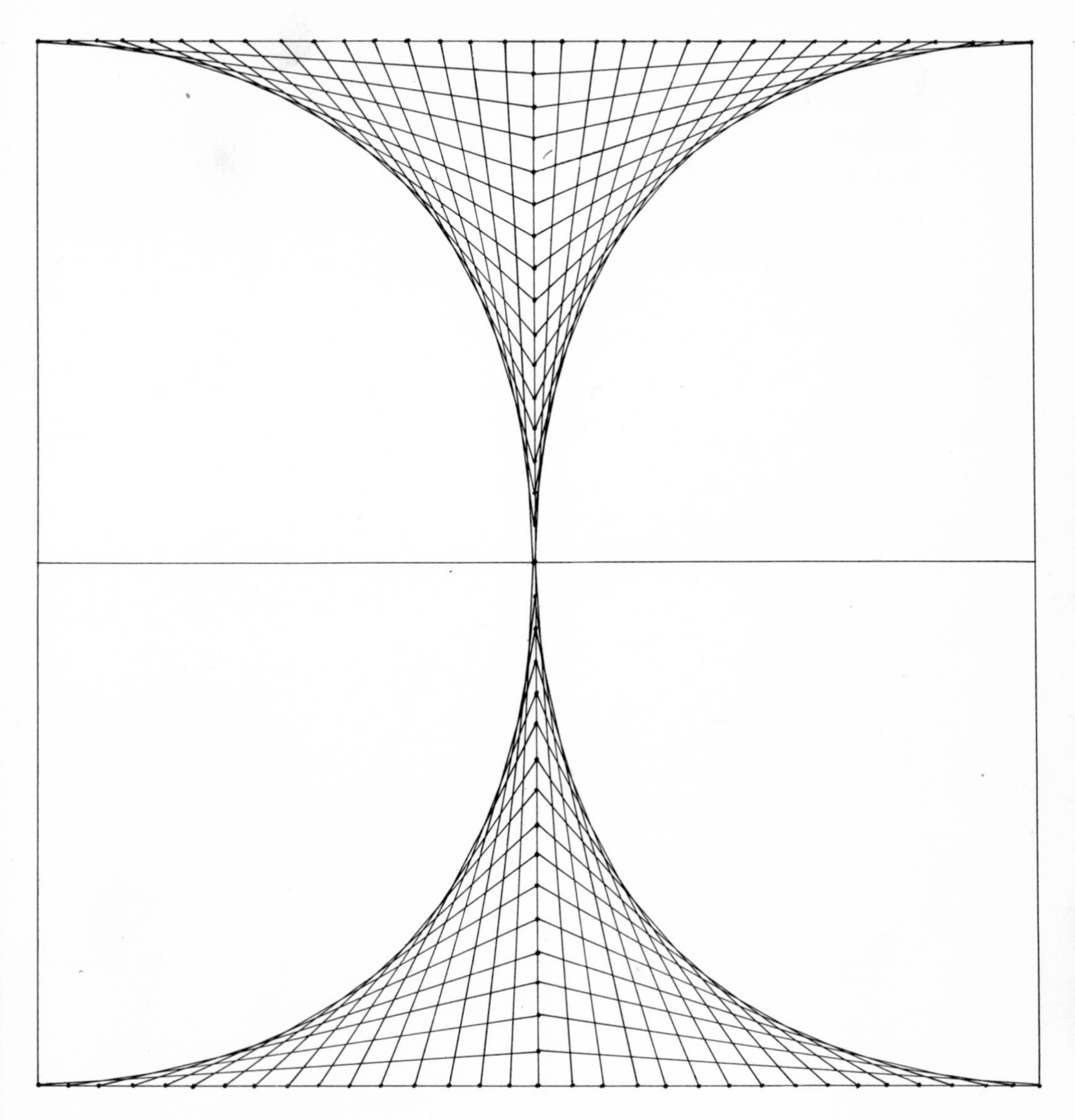

Figure 2

Design 3

1. Set up your 8-inch square exactly as you did for the last two designs.
2. Using the same method you used in Design 2, work each new angle marked with an x.
3. Figure 2 is the finished design.

Figure 1

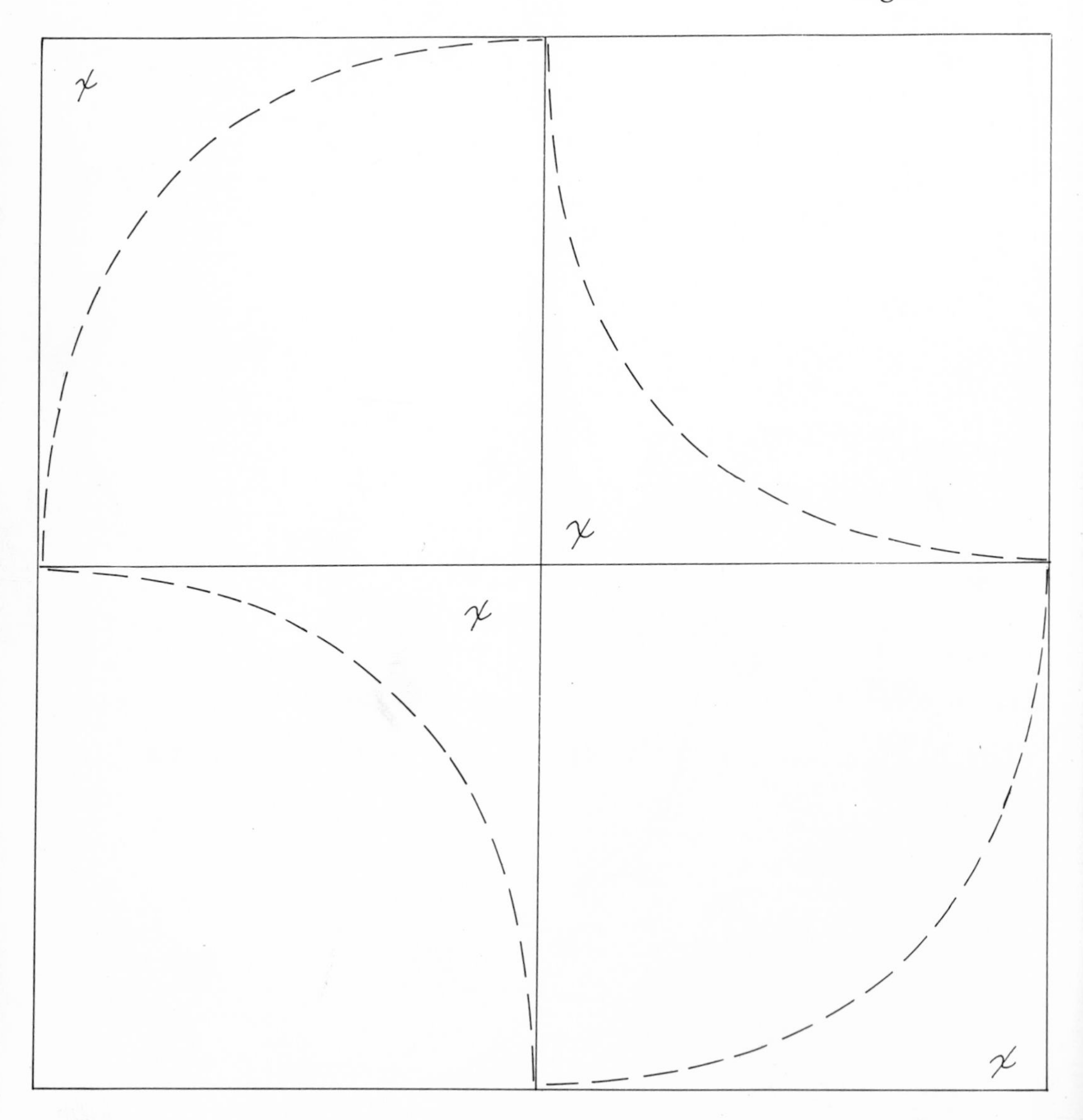

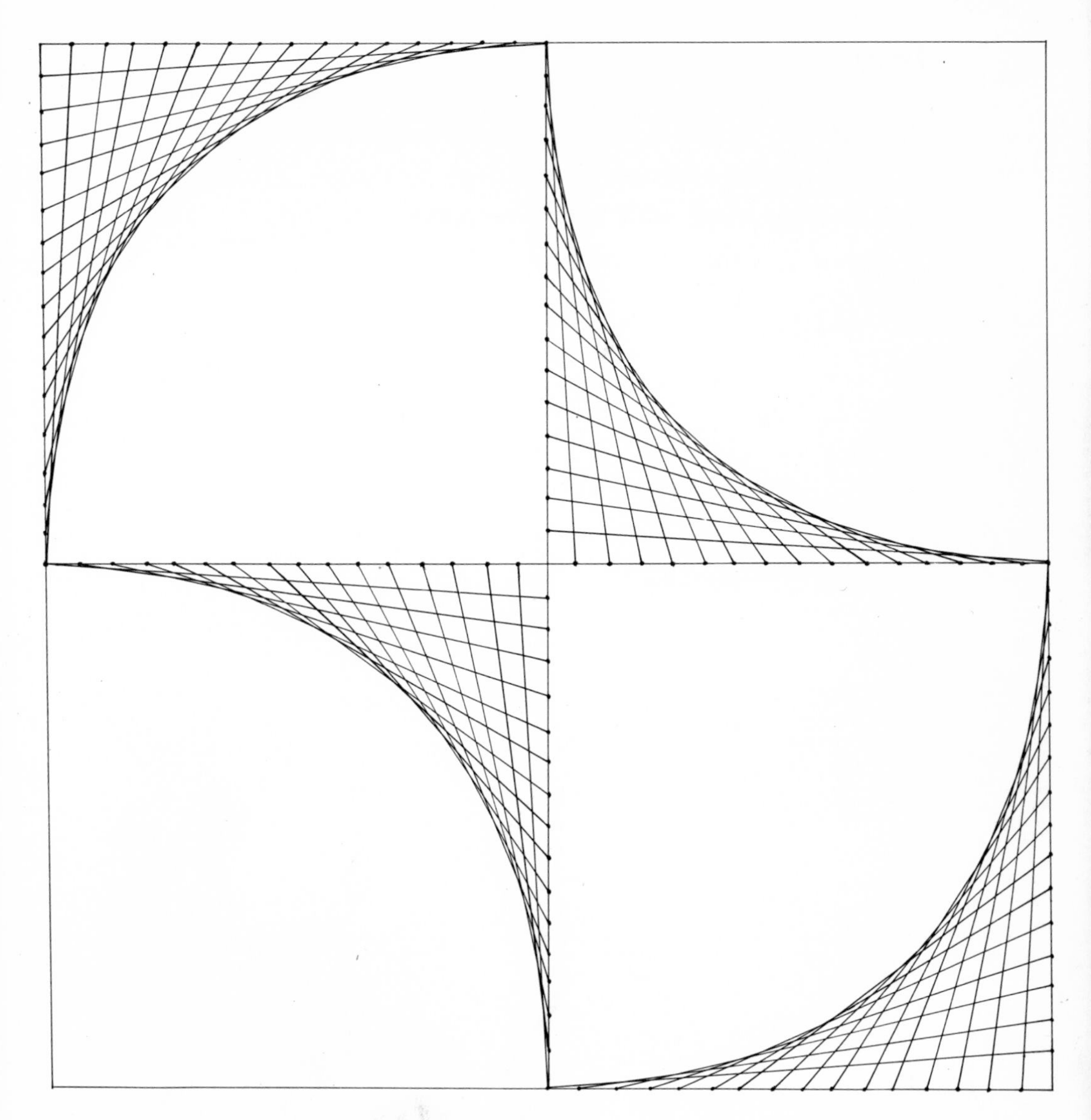

Figure 2

Design 4

1. Make your 8-inch square and divide it into four 4-inch squares. Put in the dots, as you did previously.

2. Work all the angles marked x.

3. The completed design has the "eyes" touching the center.

Figure 1

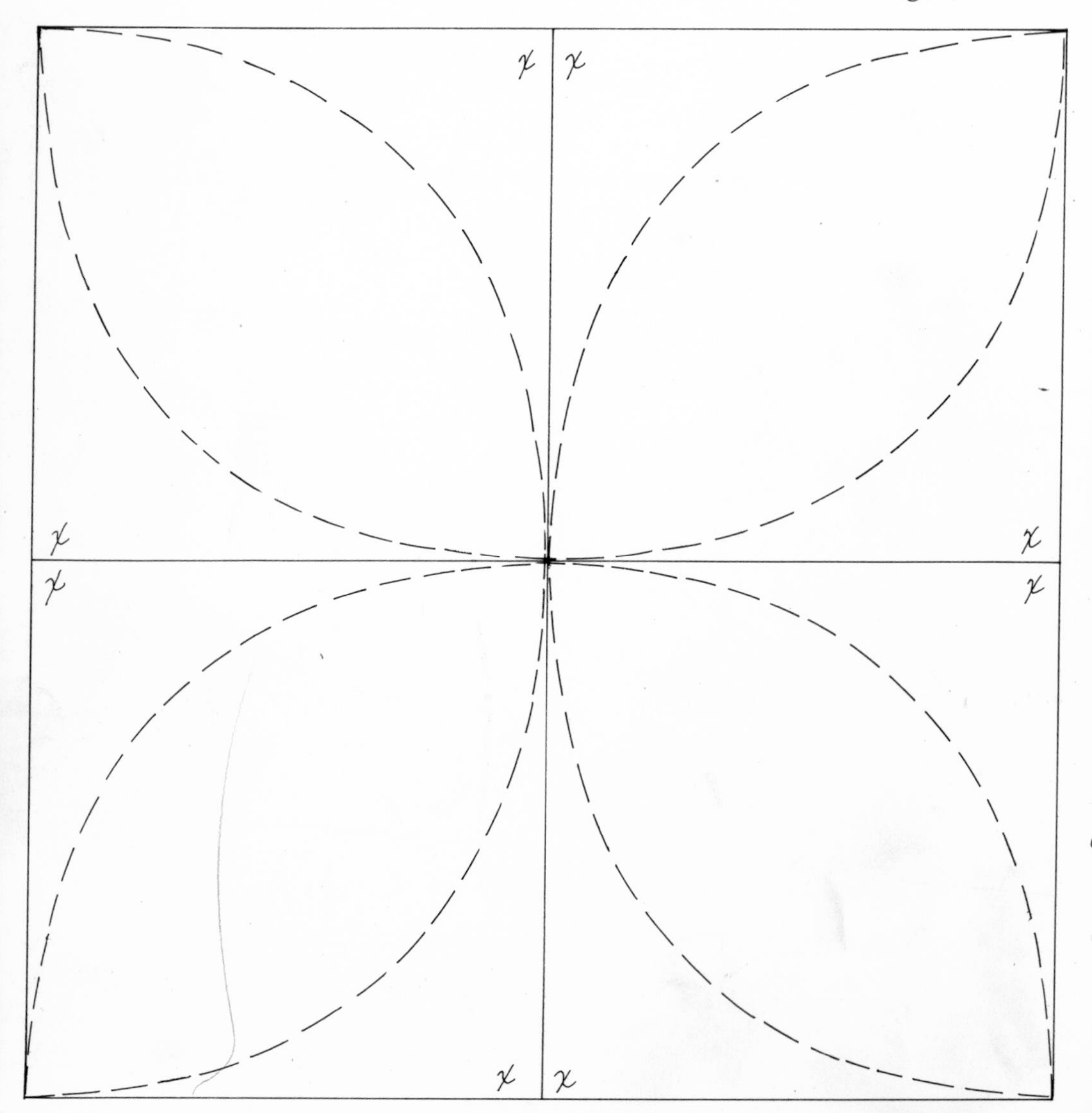

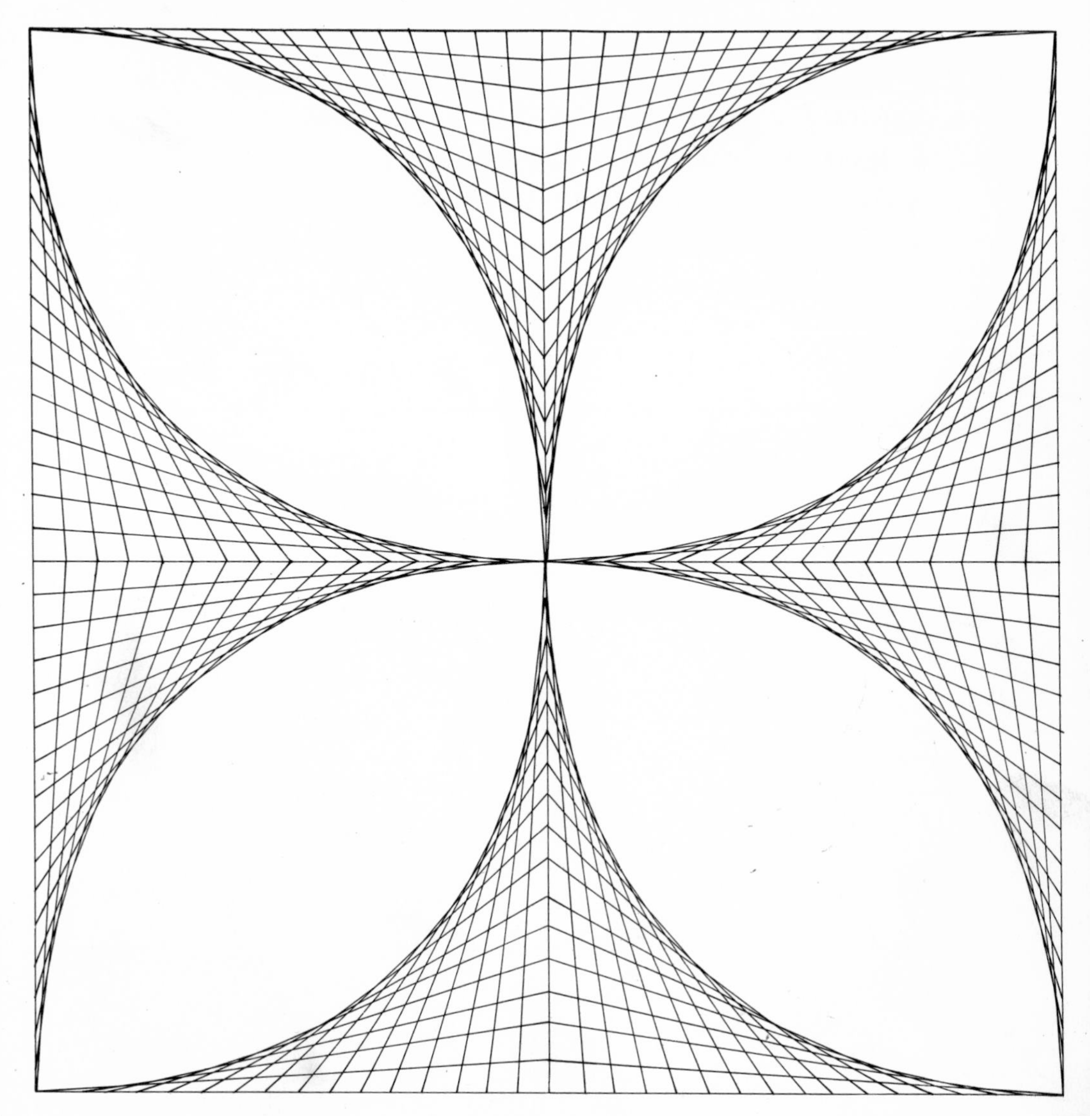

Figure 2

Design 5

1. Make your 8-inch square, divide it into four 4-inch squares, and put in your dots.

2. Work all the angles marked x. Notice how the lines overlap one another. (Cover three of the 4-inch squares and see a new design, which would be a good one all by itself.)

Notice how many of your lines had to go over others. Be

Figure 1

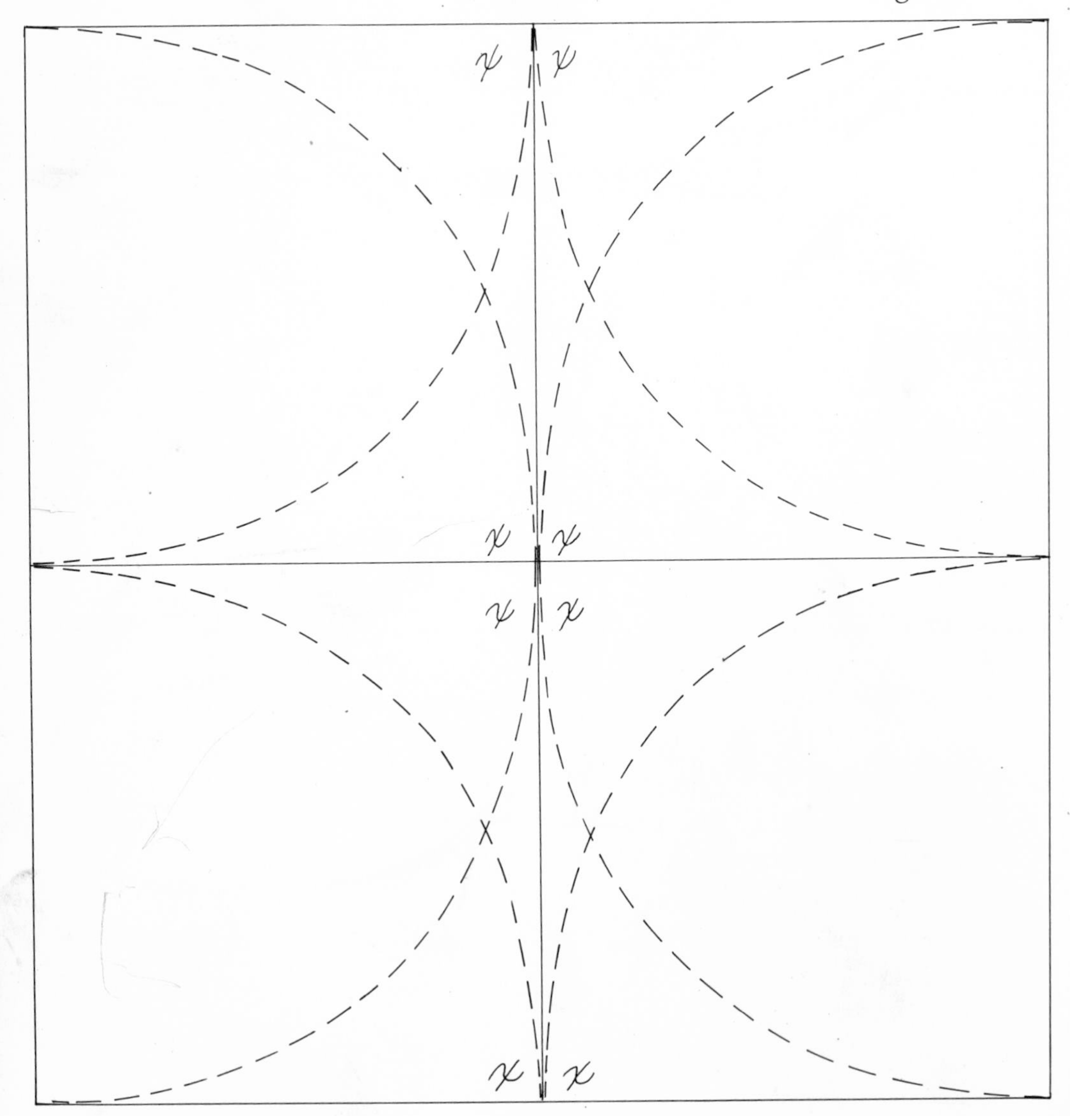

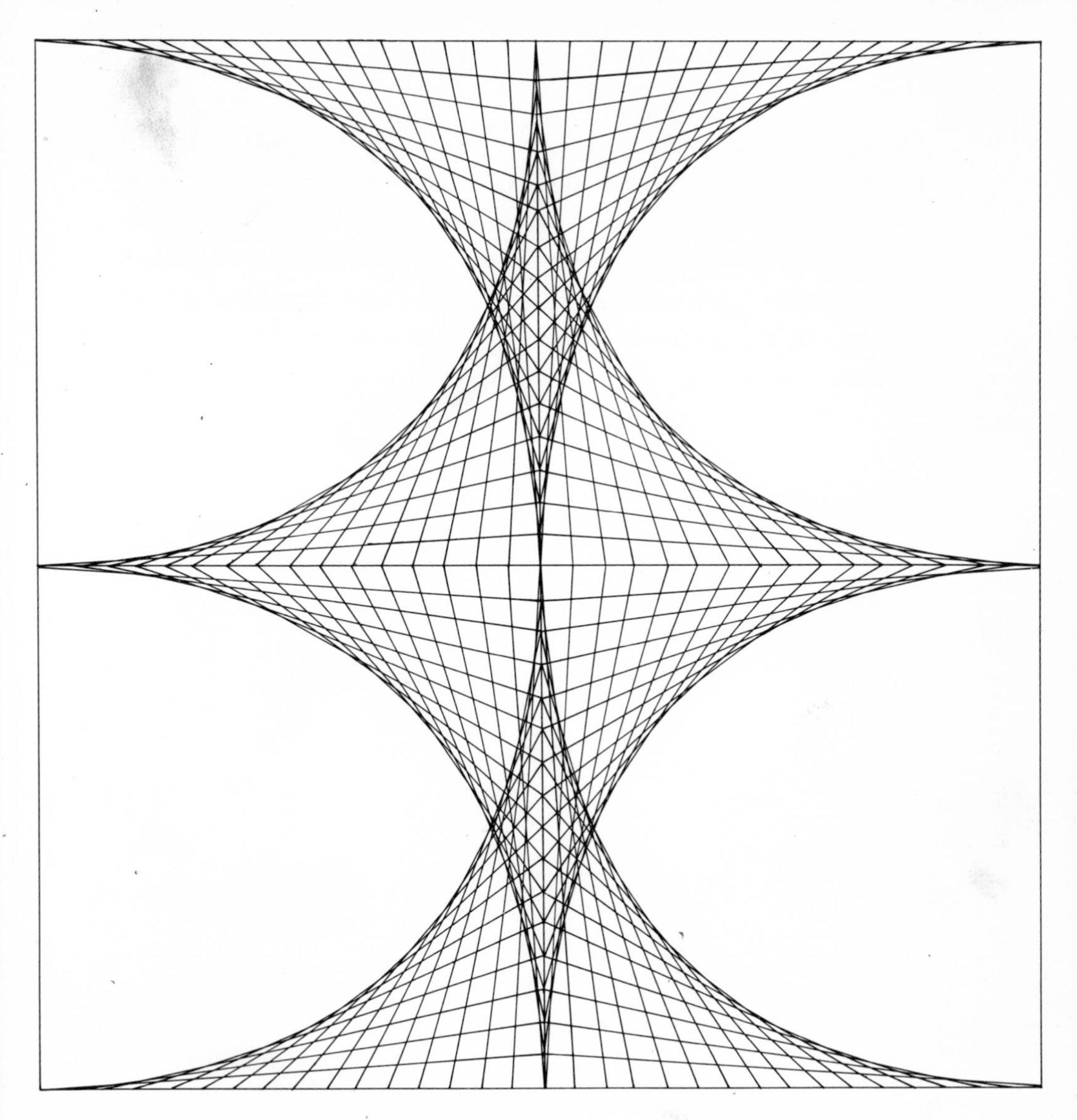

Figure 2

very careful when you cross other lines. Concentrate on connecting the right dots. Let the lines crossing over each other take care of themselves. *You watch the dots!*

3. Figure 2 is the finished design. Hold it away from you. Do you see an additional darker design where the lines crossed each other?

You can create a great number of different designs by varying the number and sizes of the squares. You can make 8-inch squares, divided into 4-inch squares, and decide which angles you want to work and which ones you will leave as they are. If you prefer, you can try designs with more than four 4-inch squares, filling in the angles of your choice.

More Designs

Combining Different Lengths

Using lines of different lengths will produce still different curves. Try this one.

1. Make your 90-degree angle, with one line 8 inches long and the other 4 inches long.

2. On the 8-inch line put the dots ½-inch apart; on the 4-inch line put them ¼-inch apart. This will give you the same number of dots on each line.

3. Connect the dots as you did before.

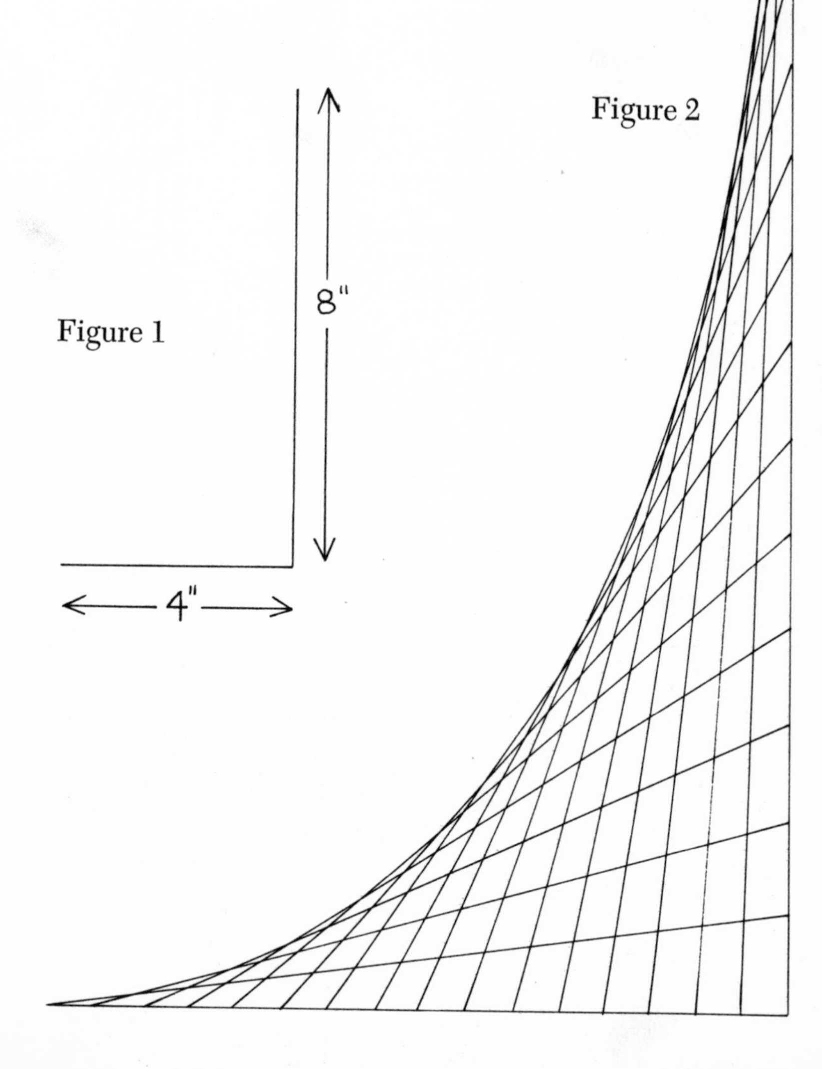

Figure 1

Figure 2

Try the same design in reverse.

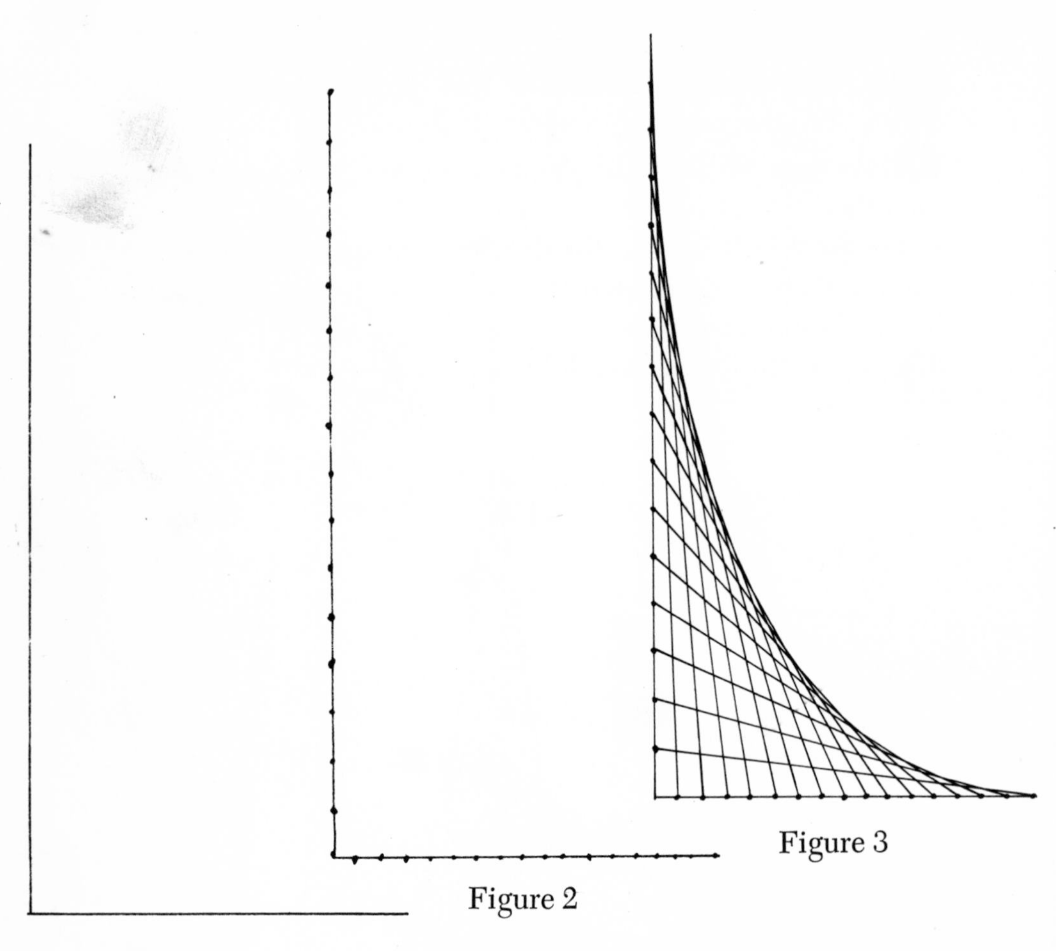

Figure 1

Figure 2

Figure 3

Designs Back-to-Back

Make the same two designs you just did, but put them back-to-back. One 8-inch arm will be used for both, but the base, also 8 inches long, will be divided in half to give you two 4 inch arms.

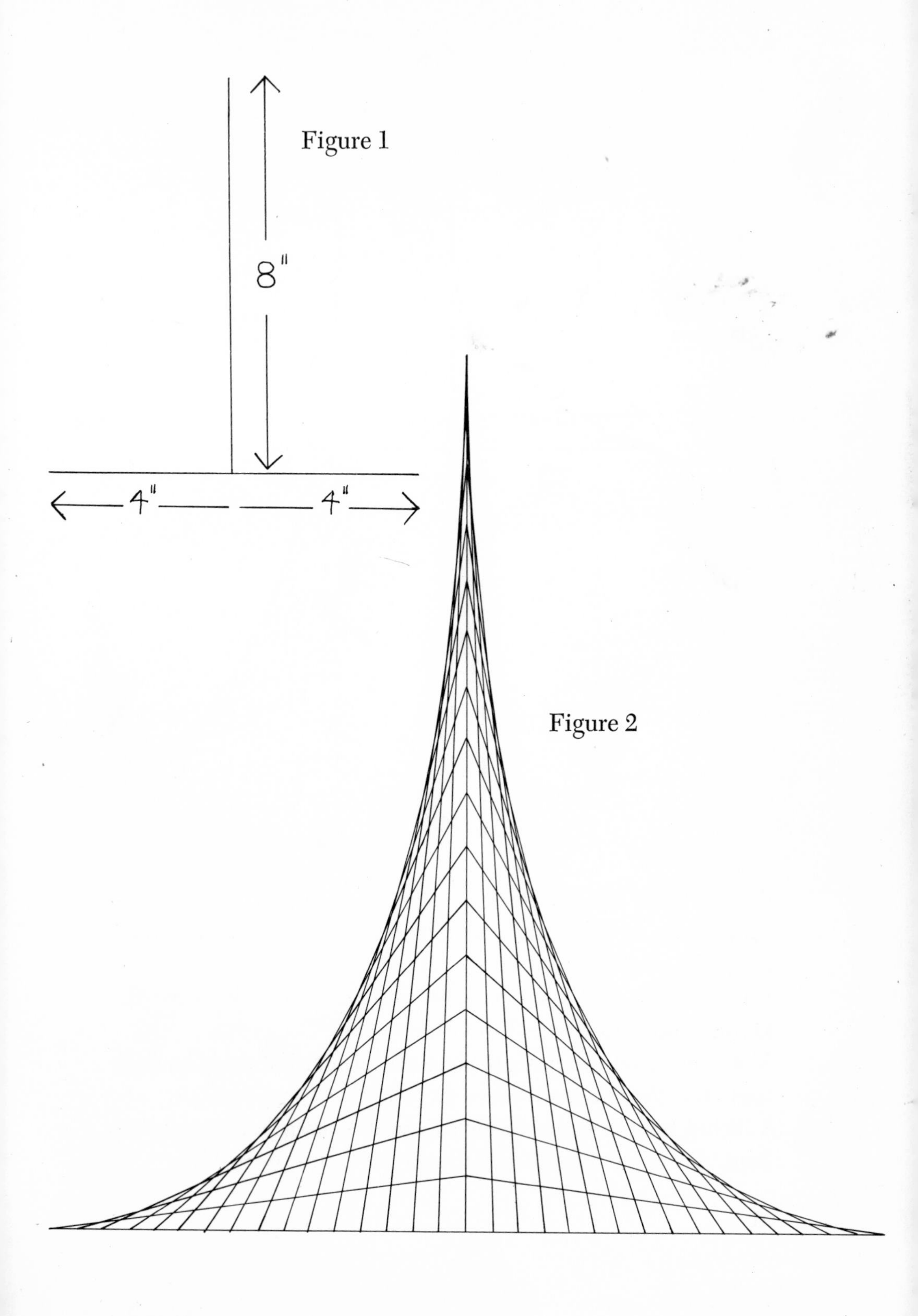

Figure 1

Figure 2

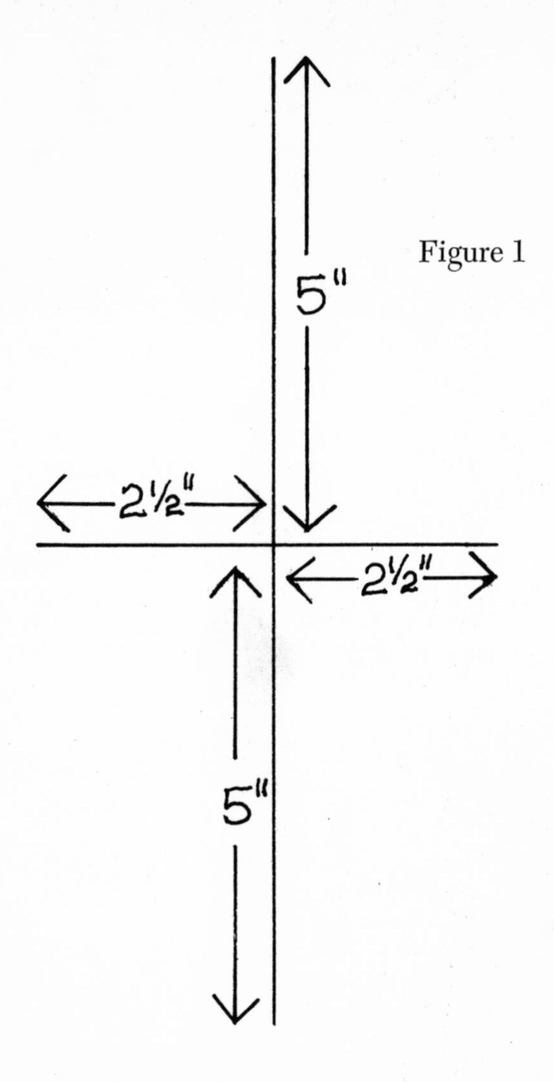

Figure 1

Shorter Arms Back-to-Back

This design is made by putting the last design back-to-back along the shorter arms.

1. Draw four angles so that they are back-to-back; make the longer arms 5 inches and the shorter ones 2½ inches.

2. Put the dots ½-inch apart on the 5-inch lines and ¼-inch apart on the 2½-inch lines.

3. Work the top two sections as you did the preceding design. Turn the paper upside down and finish the design.

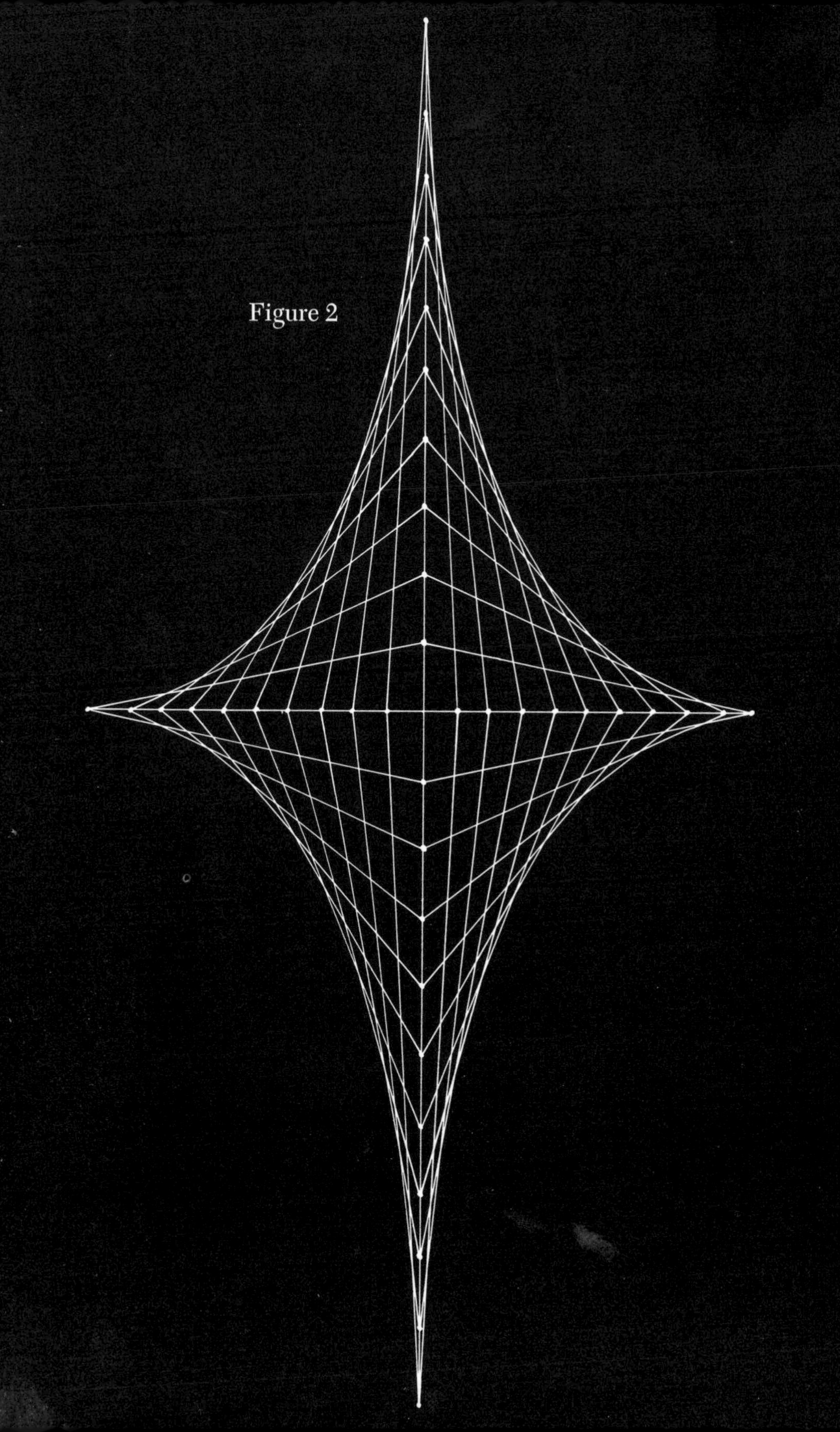

Figure 2

Overlapping Lines

The following design lets the lines overlap each other, showing a darker pattern in the center.

1. Draw two 90-degree angles back-to-back, making the vertical arm 8 inches long and the base arms each 4 inches long. Put the base arms close to the bottom of the paper.

2. At the top of the 8-inch arm make two more 90-degree angles, with each arm 4 inches long. Put in the dots (½-inch apart on the 8-inch line and ¼-inch on the 4-inch lines).

3. Using the two angles at the base, work them as you did in Step 3 of the last design. Turn the paper upside down and finish the design.

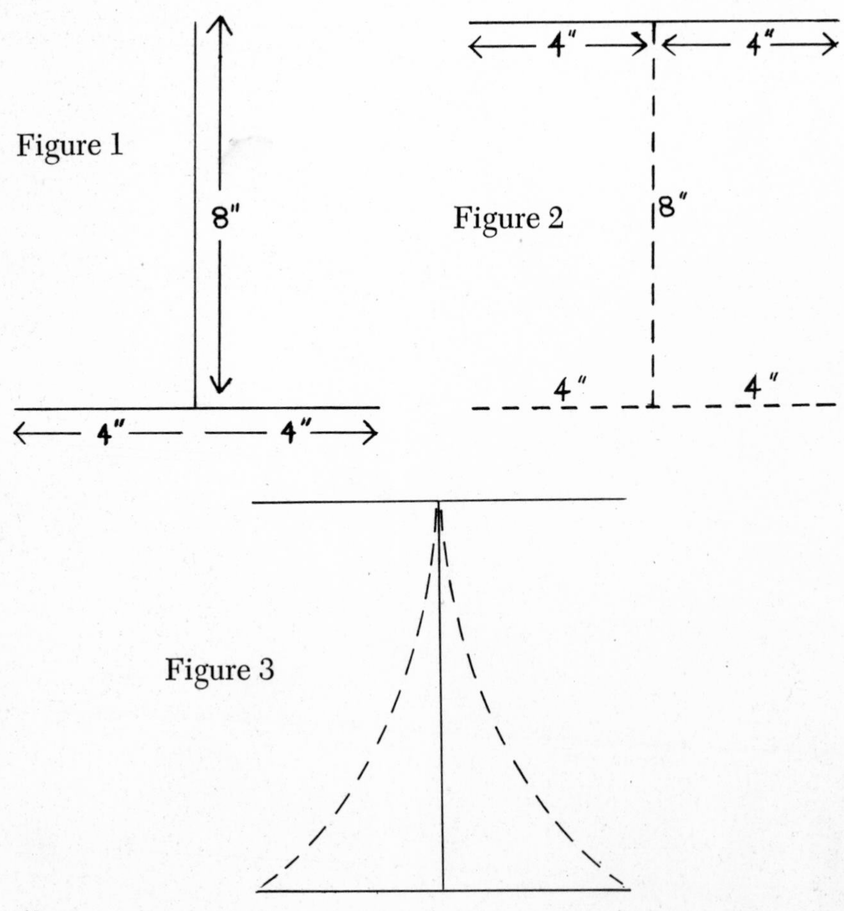

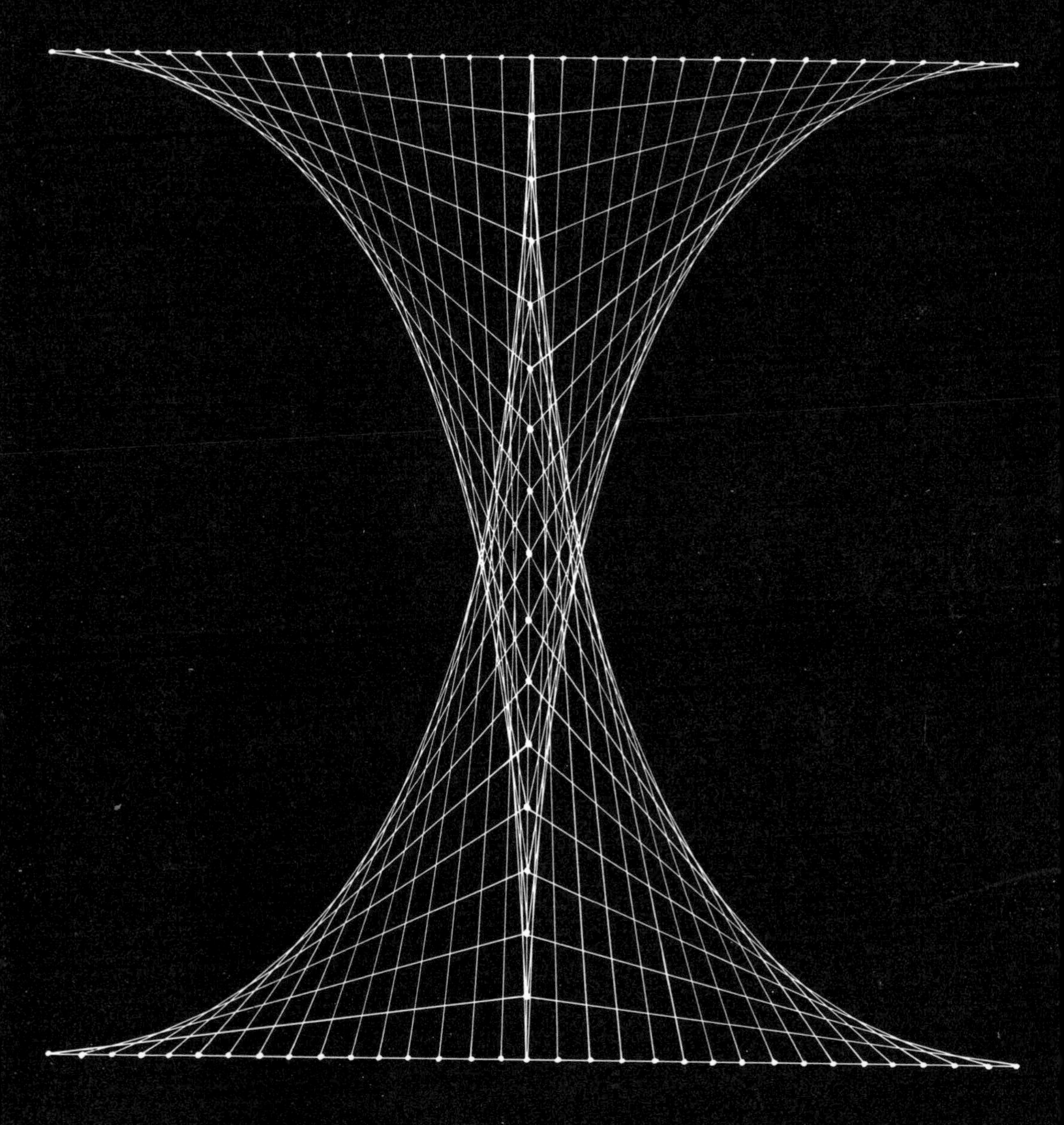

Figure 4

Combining Ideas

Try combining some of the ideas already used.

1. Starting a little below the middle of your paper, draw two 90-degree angles back-to-back, with each base arm 3 inches long and the vertical arm 6 inches long.

2. With your ruler extend the 6-inch arm 3 inches beyond the base lines. This gives you two additional 90-degree angles below the base lines, with a 3-inch long arm.

3. Mark each 3-inch arm with dots ¼-inch apart and the 6-inch arm with dots ½-inch apart.

4. Work the top two angles; turn your paper and work the others.

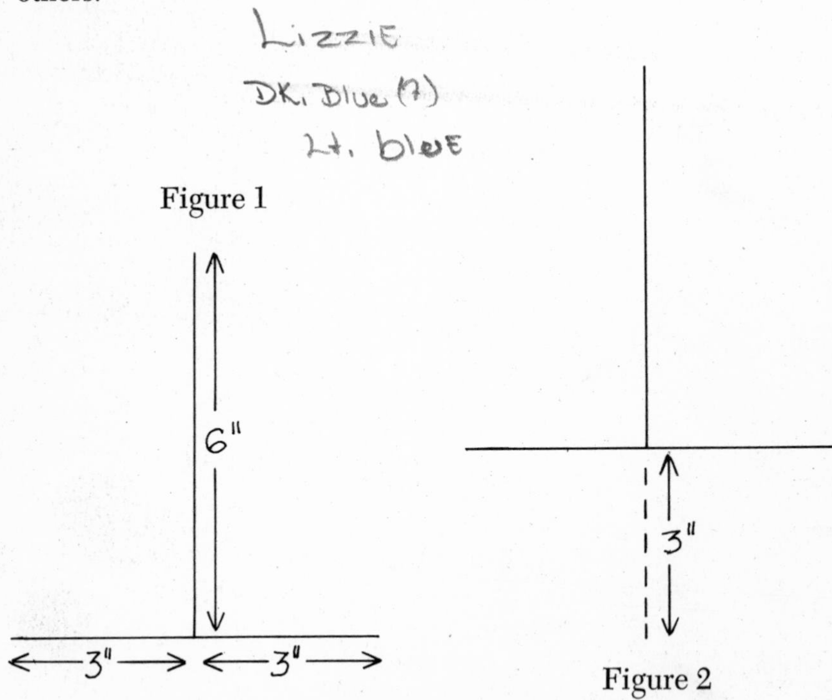

Figure 1

Figure 2

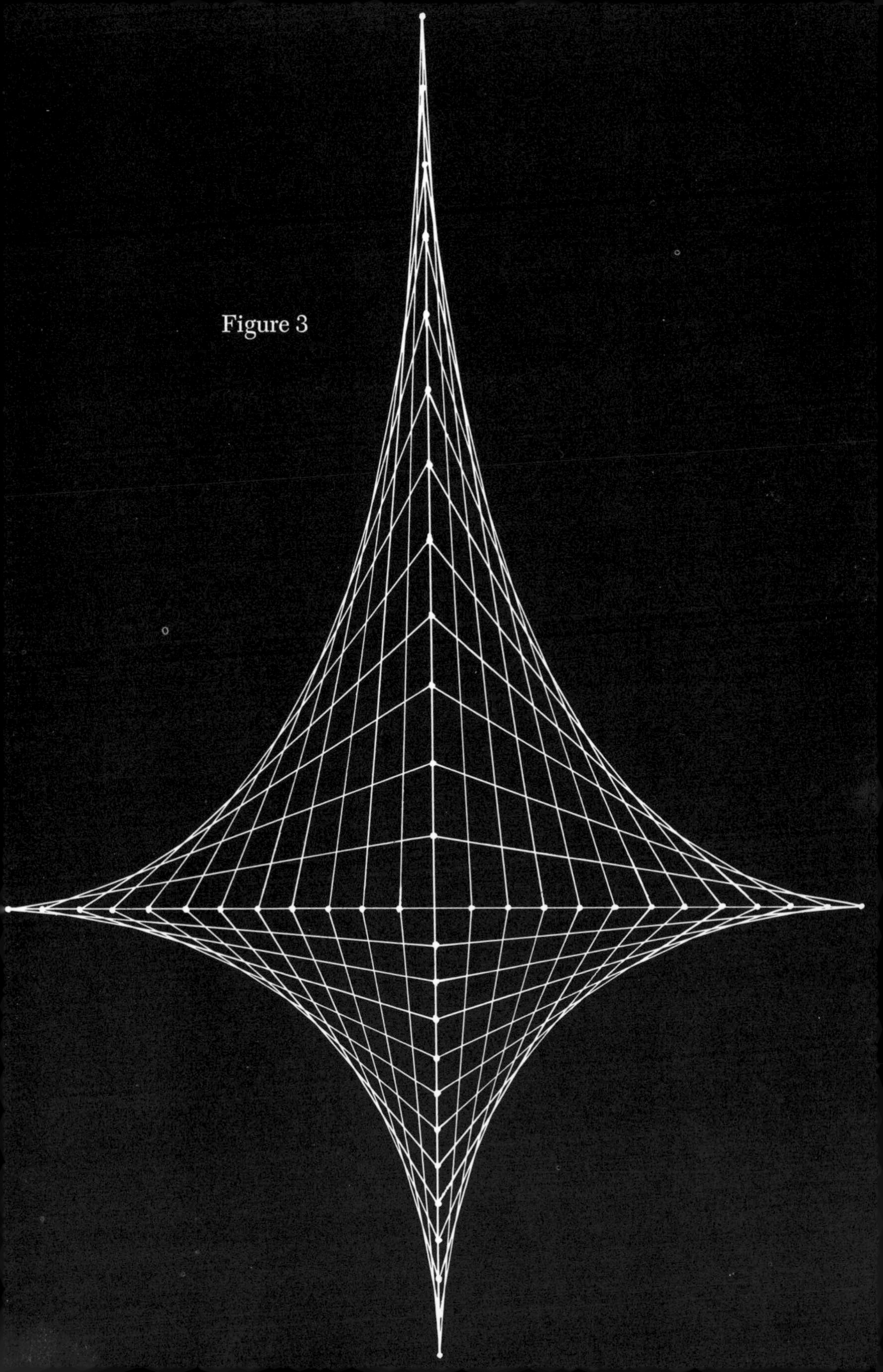
Figure 3

Angles, Angles, and More Angles

It is not always necessary to measure angles for designs—unless you want particular kinds of curves. It is necessary, however, to keep the arms straight and to have the same number of dots on each line.

The following design has eight different angles; it is easy to make a similar one.

1. Form the first angle by drawing two straight lines of the same length or making one double the length of the other. Start near the top of your paper. If the lines are the same length, use the same dot measurement on both of them. If one is double the other in length, double the dot measurement on the longer line. If your longer line is three times longer than the other, mark your dots three times farther apart. Connect your dots as you have done before.

2. Make a different angle at the outer end of one of the arms of your design. (*Watch the length of the new line so you'll know how to measure.*)

3. Connect dots on the new line with those on the "used" line that helped make your new angle.

4. Continue until you have filled your paper. Some of your lines will cross others, making your design look as if it has depth.

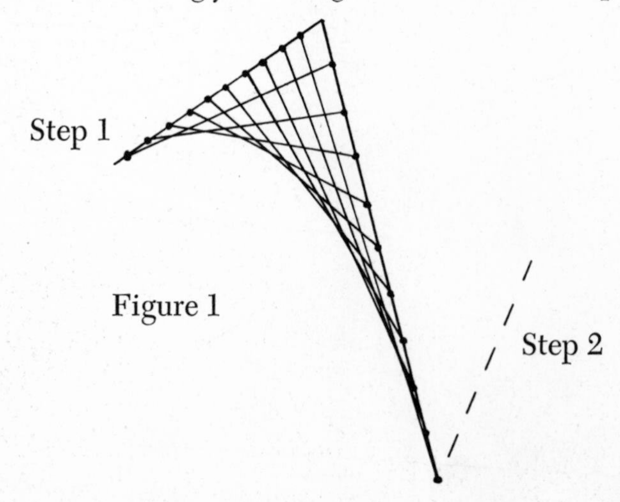

Figure 1

Working With a Circle

Sharpen your pencil for this circle design!

1. Using your ruler, draw a 6-inch line and put a dot at the halfway mark (3 inches).

2. Lay your protractor along the base line, as you learned to do it on page 17. Carefully trace around the curved edge of the protractor, making a half-circle. Stop at the base lines.

3. Before removing the protractor, put dots at the 30, 60, 90, 120, and 150 degree markings. Also put a dot at each end of the base line.

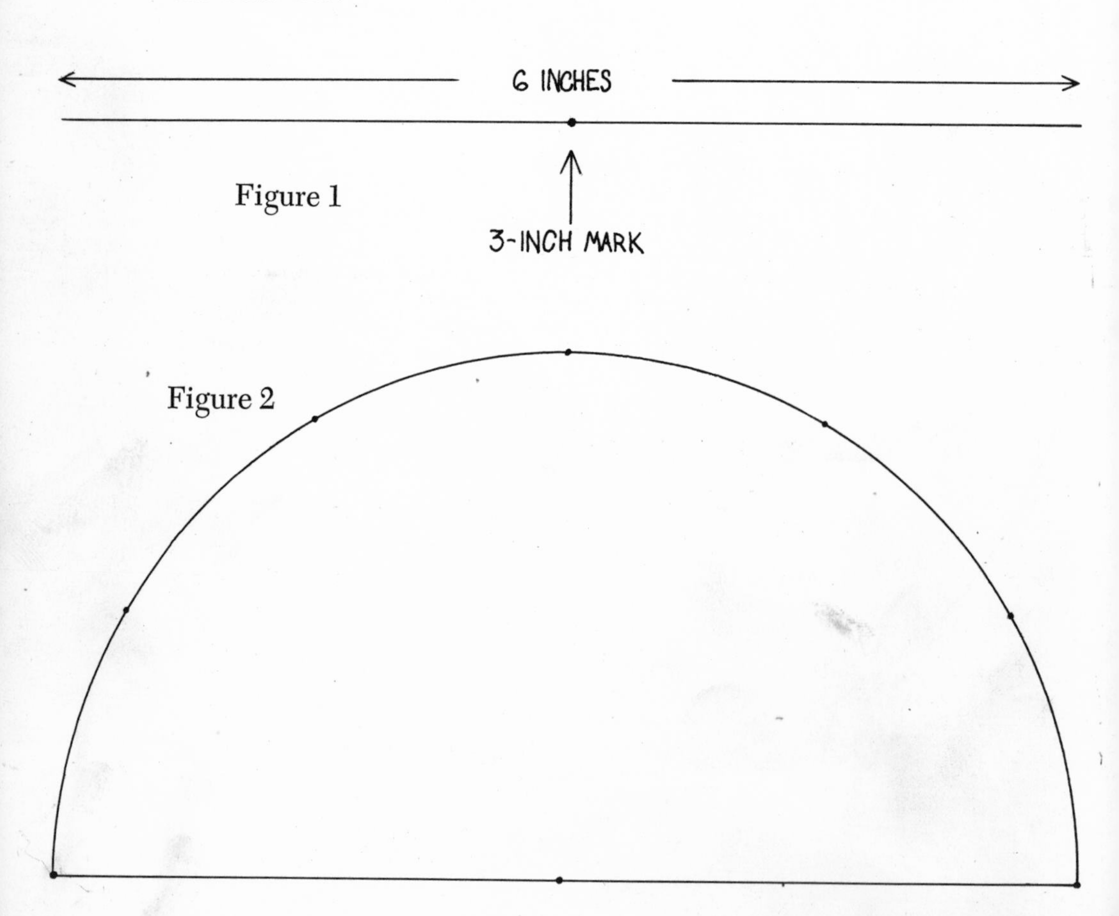

Figure 1

Figure 2

4. Turn the figure upside-down and repeat Steps 2 and 3—making a perfect circle with twelve dots equally spaced around the circle.

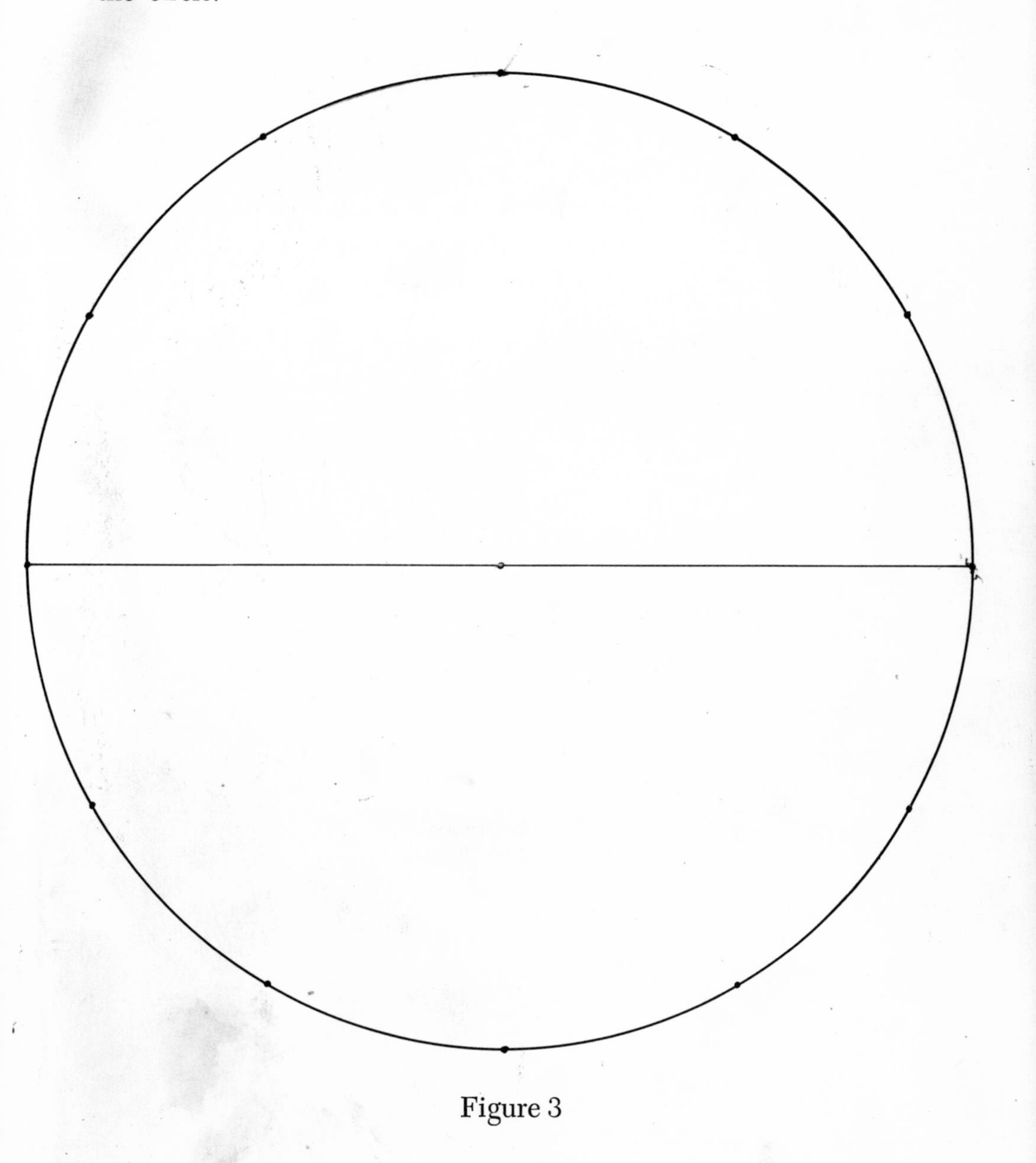

Figure 3

5. Each dot on the circle is to be connected with a straight line to every other dot on the circle. That means lots of straight lines crossing over other straight lines.

6. Connect the first dot with all the other dots on the circle.

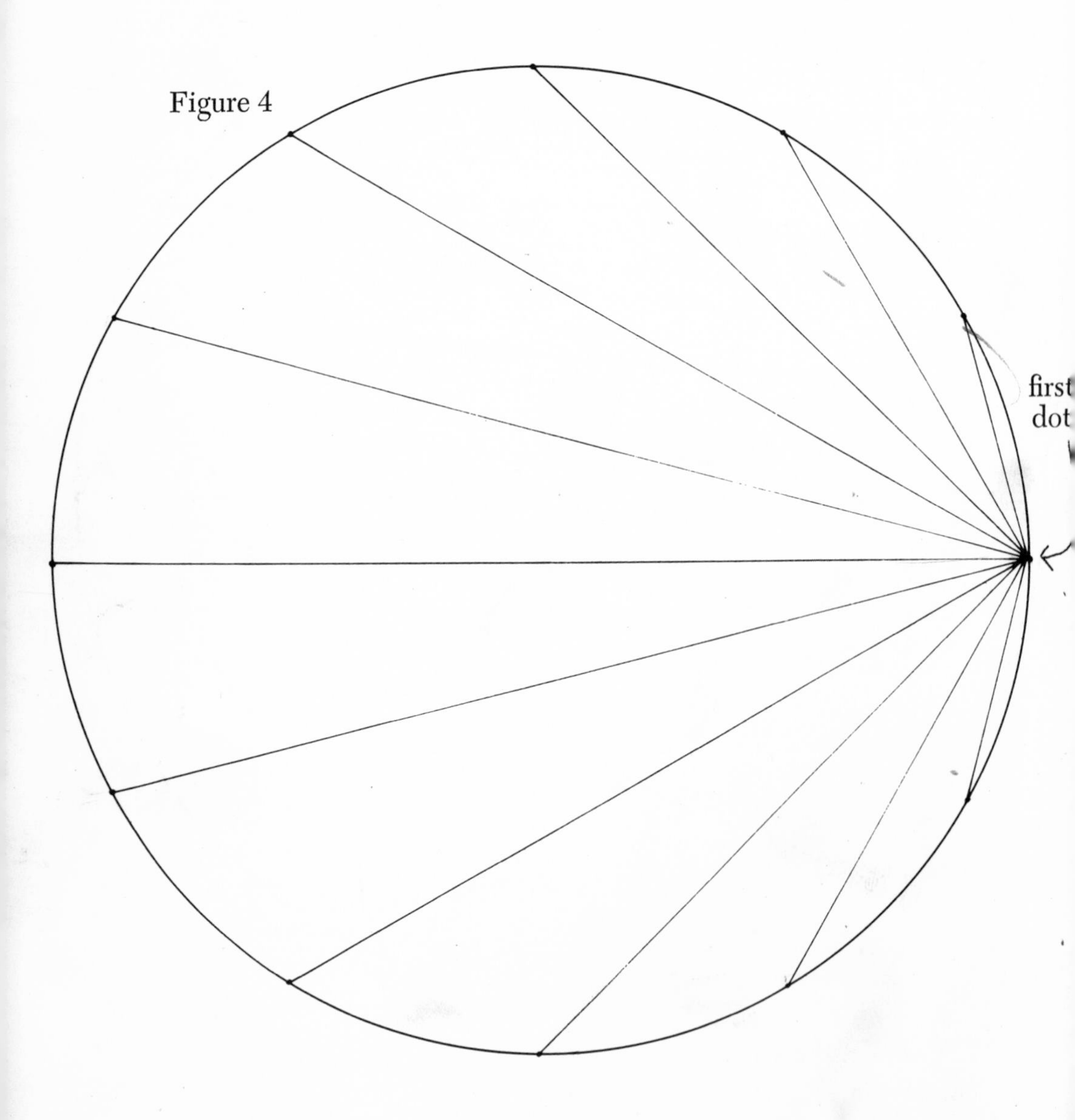

Figure 4

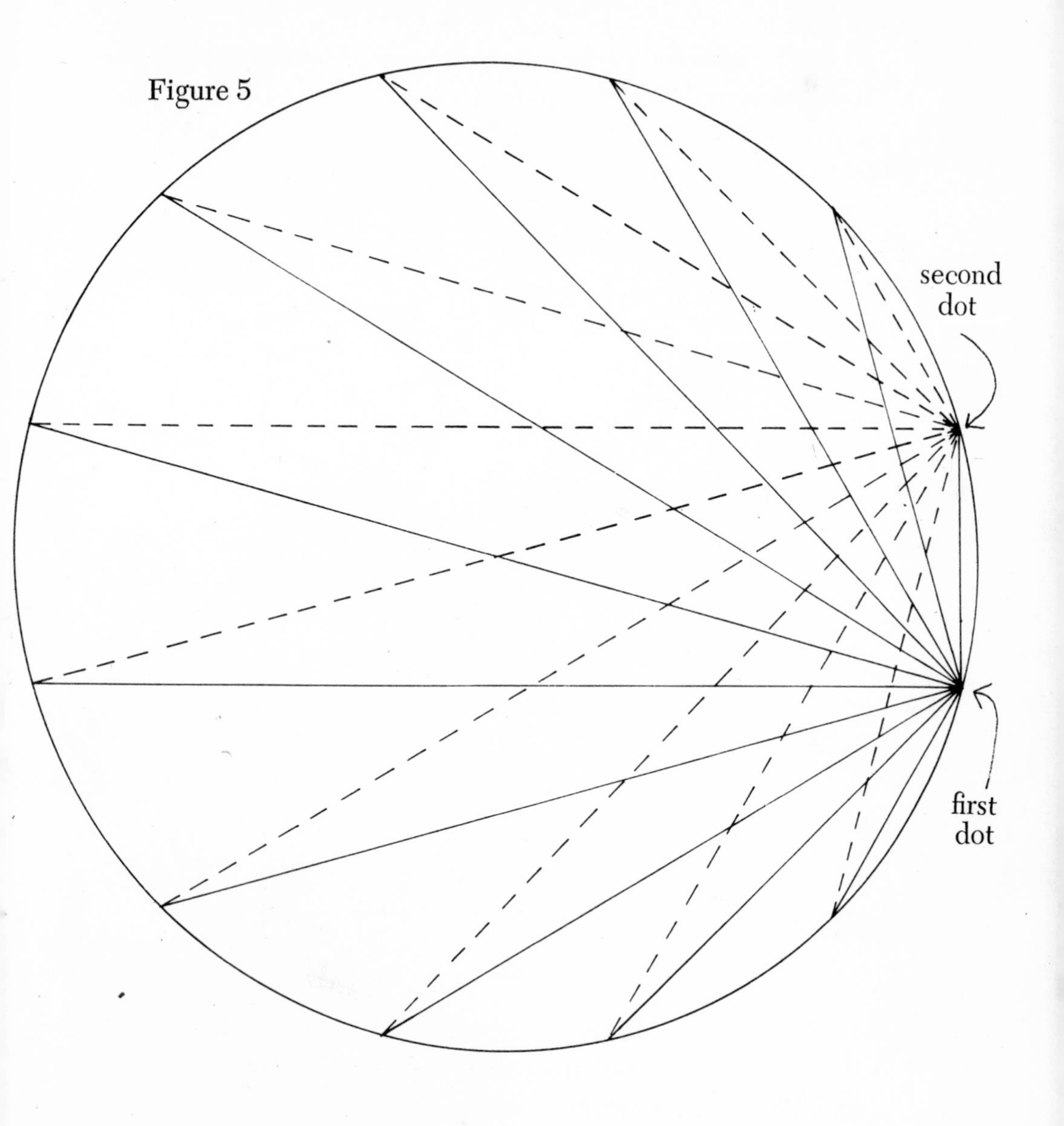

7. Connect the second dot with all the other dots on the circle (broken line).

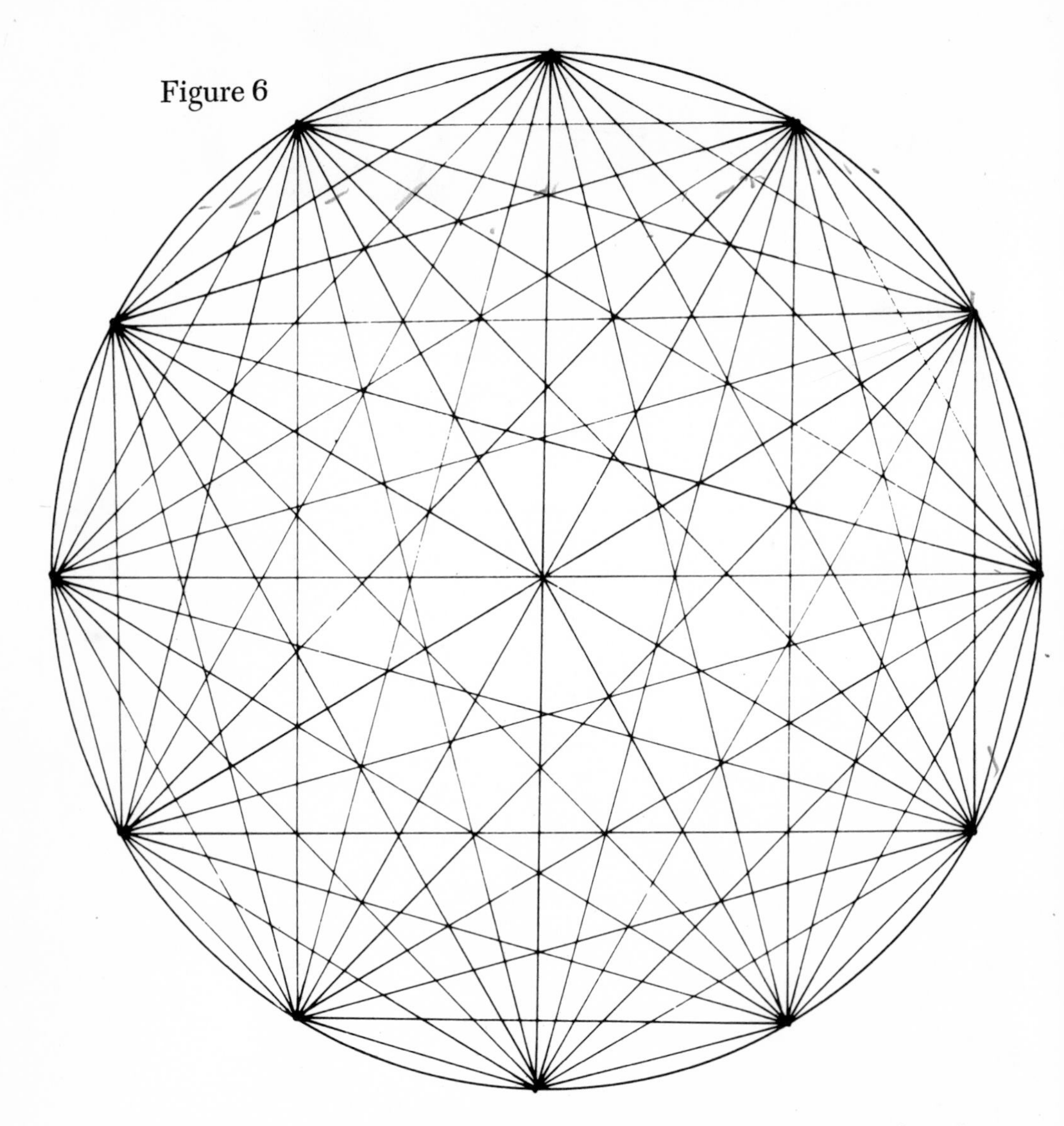
Figure 6

8. Continue around the circle until each dot is connected with the other dots around the circle. Here's what your design will look like if you work *very carefully.*

If you want eighteen dots instead of twelve, put your dots around the curve of the protractor at 20, 40, 60, 80, 100, 120, 140, and 160, and at the base lines. Then connect *each* dot with *all* the other dots on the circle. Dots at 15 or 10 degree intervals will make still different designs.

Curved Lines

The designs in this chapter start with a curved line.

1. Draw a half circle with your protractor and put a dot at each 5-degree mark around the outer edge (from B to C).

2. Turn the curved edge of the protractor down. Proceed as above, completing the circle and placing the dots 5 degrees apart. There should be 72 dots on the circle.

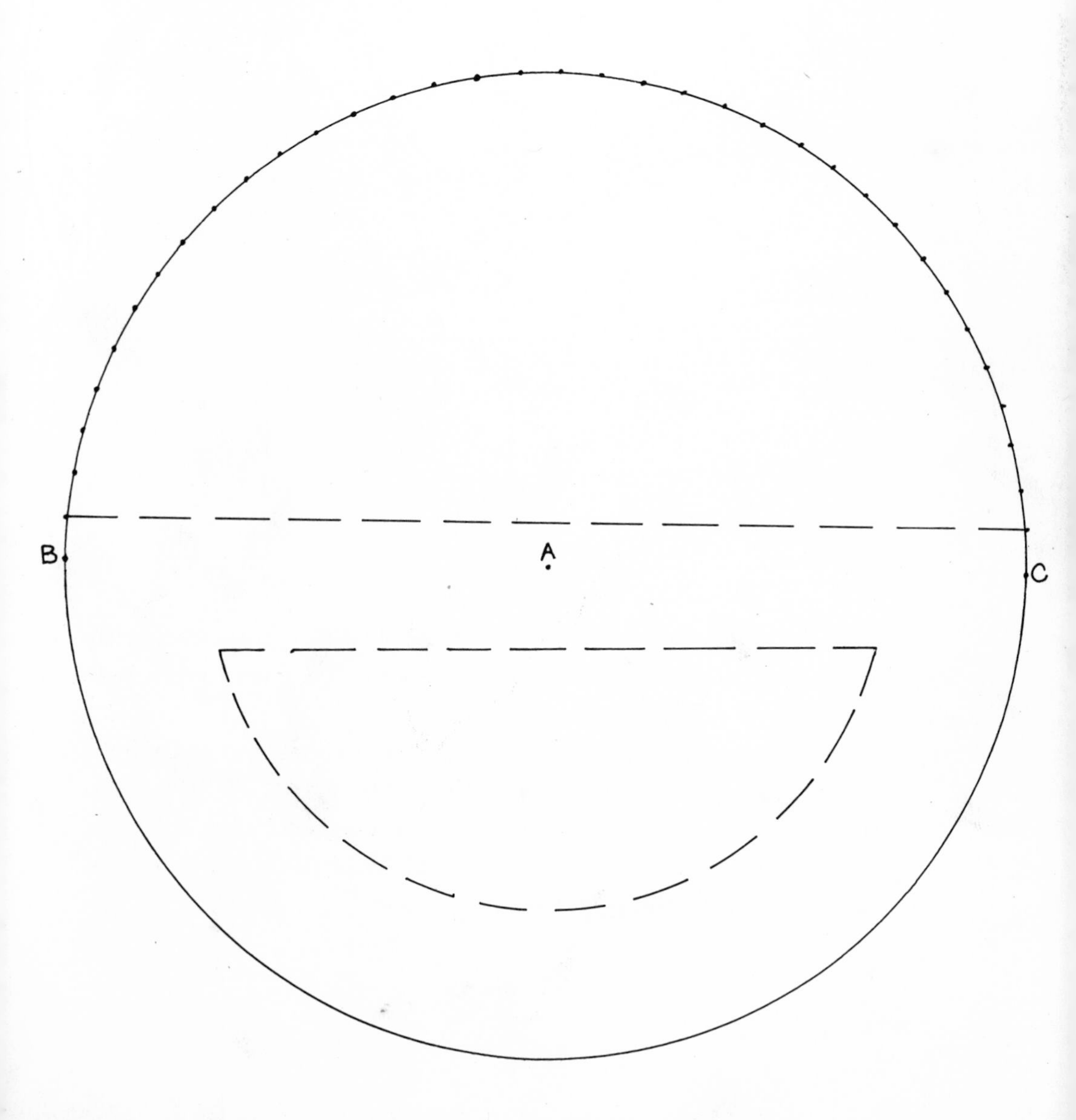

3. Starting at the top of the circle, letter your first five dots A, B, C, D, and E, going down the right side of the circle.
4. Count down twenty more dots, and letter that dot A^1. Letter the next four dots B^1, C^1, D^1, and E^1.
5. With your ruler connect your A and A^1. Connect the B's, C's, D's, and E's the same way.

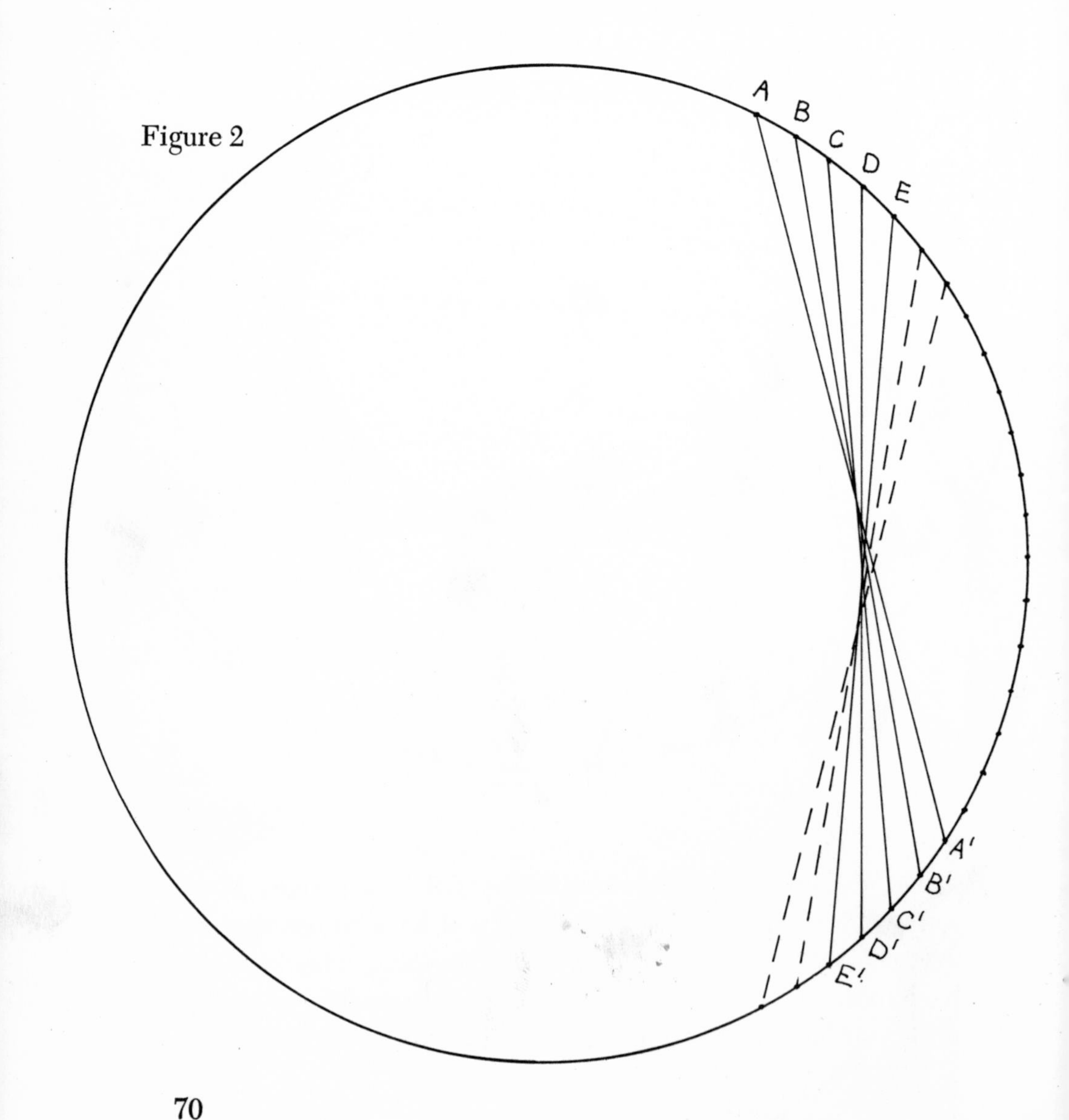

Figure 2

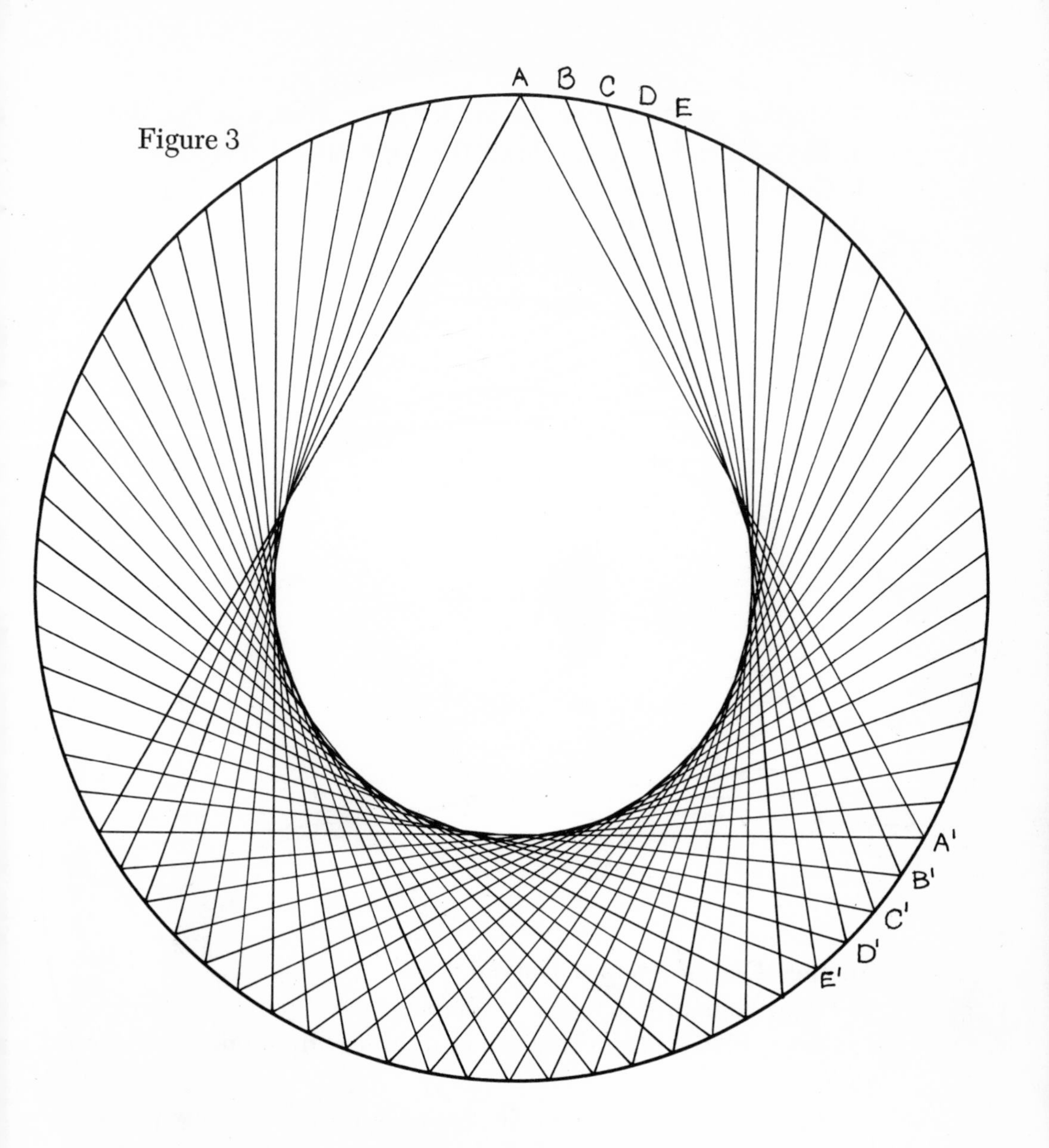

6. Go around the circle, using the next dot each time. When you get to the place marked A[1], you will have to use that dot again. Continue around your circle, stopping when you get back to the A, making a teardrop design; or you may go around until you have used each dot twice, making a circle inside.

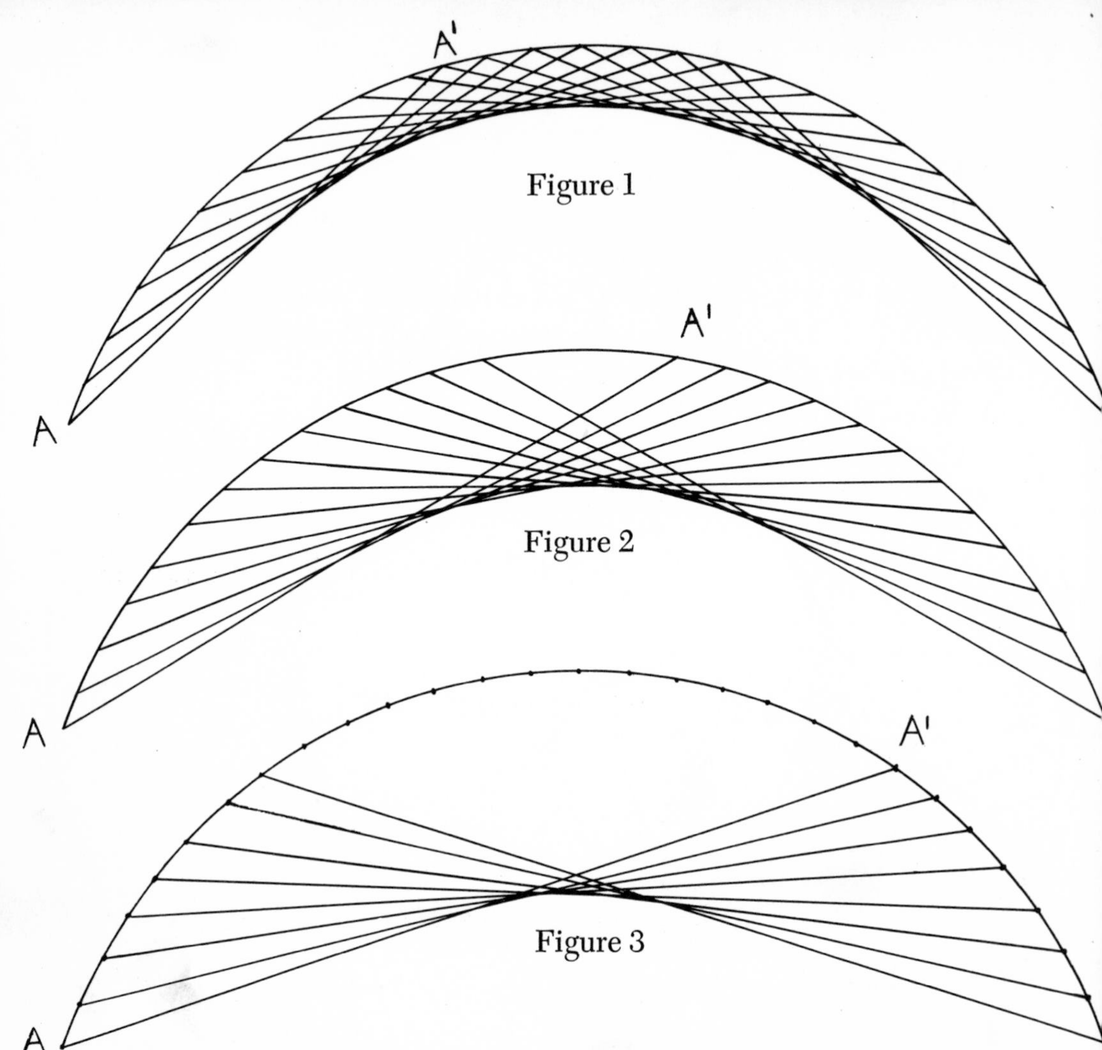

Figure 1

Figure 2

Figure 3

Another Design From a Curved Line

1. Using your protractor or a compass, draw part of a circle (an arc). Place your dots at equal distances from one another along the arc.

2. Mark your first dot A. Move along your arc about one-third of its full distance and mark that dot A^1.

3. Connect A and A^1; continue as you did with your circle. The design will be finished when you have used the last dot on the arc.

4. For variations with arcs of the same size, start your A^1 dot at a different place (see Figures 2 and 3).

A Fish

1. Position two arcs so that they meet at one end and cross each other near the other end.

2. Put in equally spaced dots. Label one "tail" dot A. About one-third of the way around the arc mark A^1. Connect the two marked dots, and finish the arc.

3. Work the other arc the same way.

For a different fish design: start as you did in Step 2. Continue around both arcs until you have used all the dots.

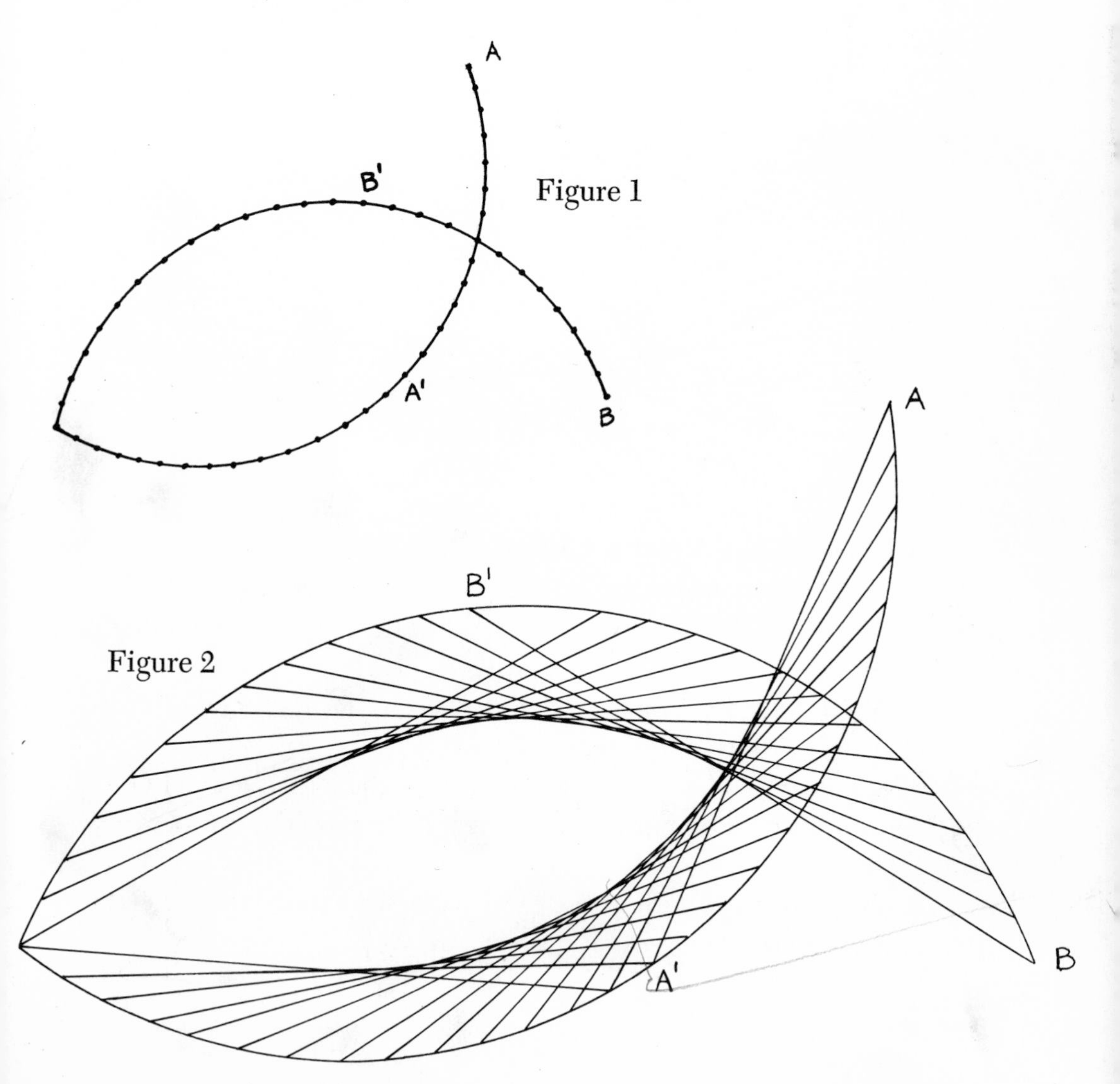

Figure 1

Figure 2

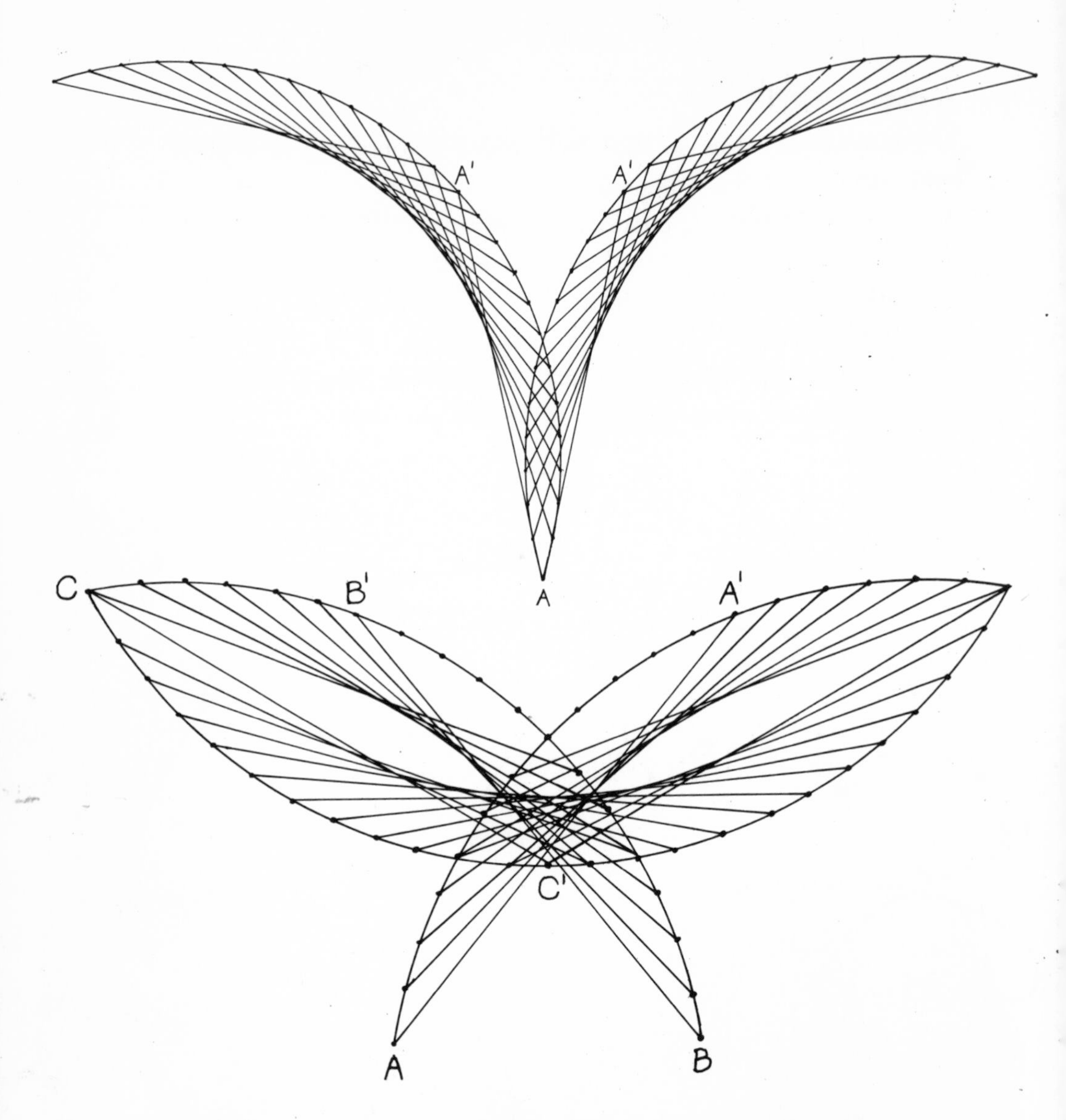

A Bird

1. Draw two arcs as shown in the diagram and put in the dots.
2. Proceed as in Step 2 when making the fish.

A Butterfly

1. Draw three arcs as shown in the diagram.
2. Put in equally spaced dots, label them, and connect them.

Scribble Design

Designs can be made from scribbles as well as from angles and arcs.

1. Draw a scribble, but keep it simple. Join the ends.

2. Put in equally spaced dots, and mark one of the dots A. Moving several inches from A, mark A^1.

3. Connect A and A^1. Continue to connect dots around the scribble until each dot has been used twice.

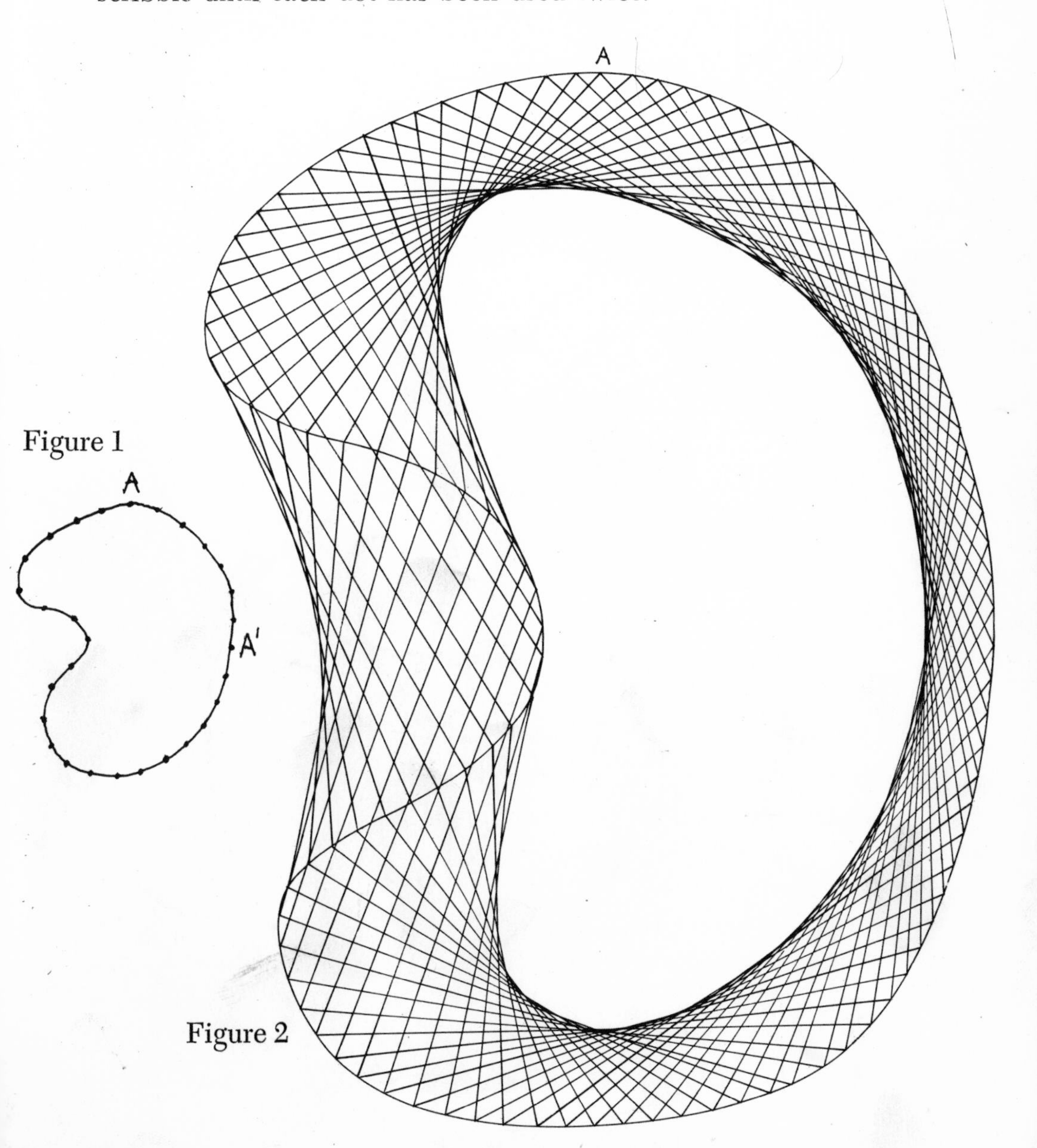

Figure 1

Figure 2

For a more complicated design, crisscross your scribbled line several times. Proceed as before.

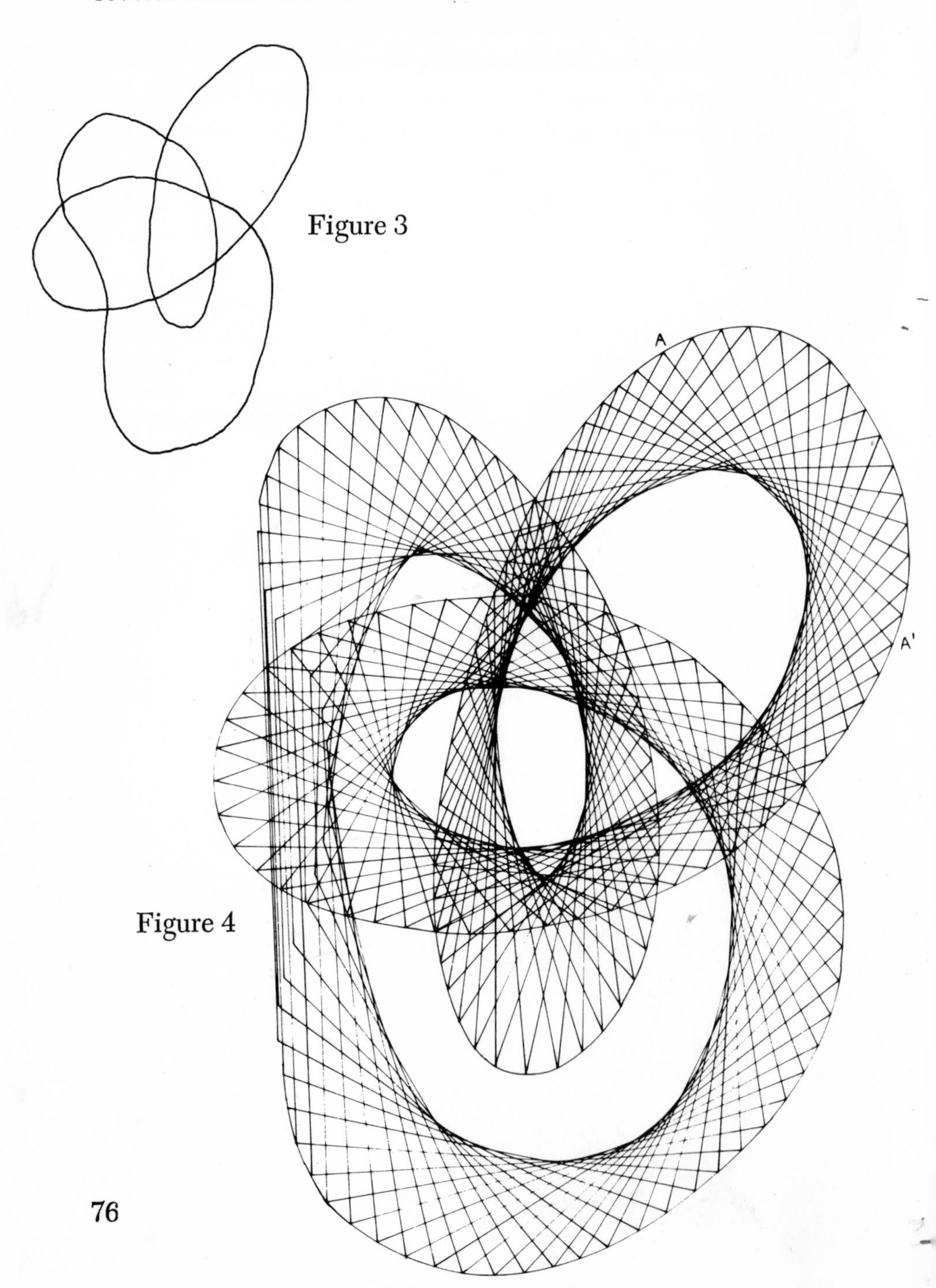

Figure 3

Figure 4

Combining Angles and Arcs

Try combining angles and arcs for some even more varied designs. The next one starts this way.

1. Arc AB and Line BC have an equal number of dots that are ¼-inch apart.

2. Line CD is half the length of Line BC. Every other dot is used on Line BC.

3. Line CD and Line DE are equal.

4. Arc EF has one more dot than Line DE.

Figure 1

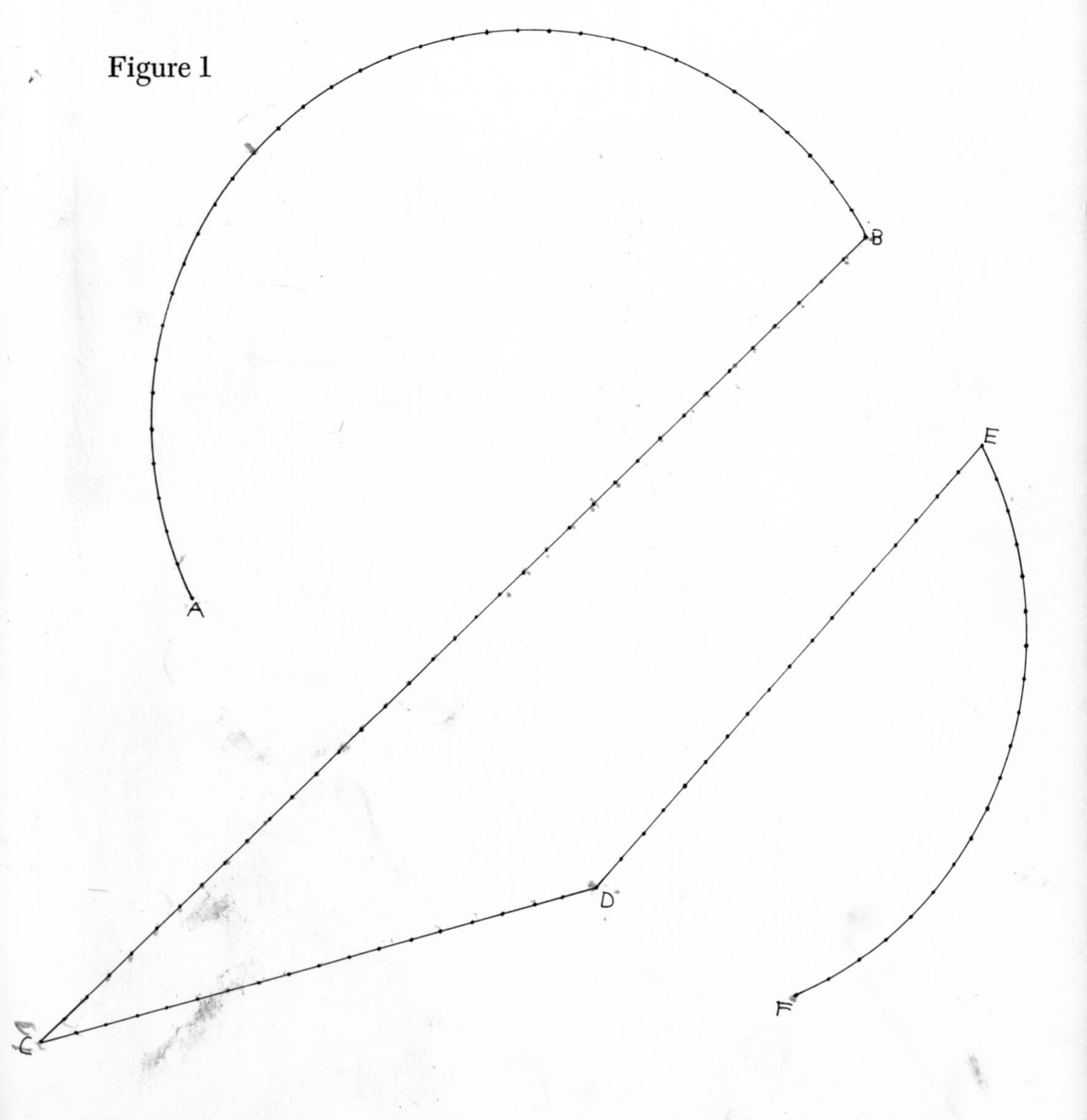

5. Broken down, the design looks like Figures 2 to 5.

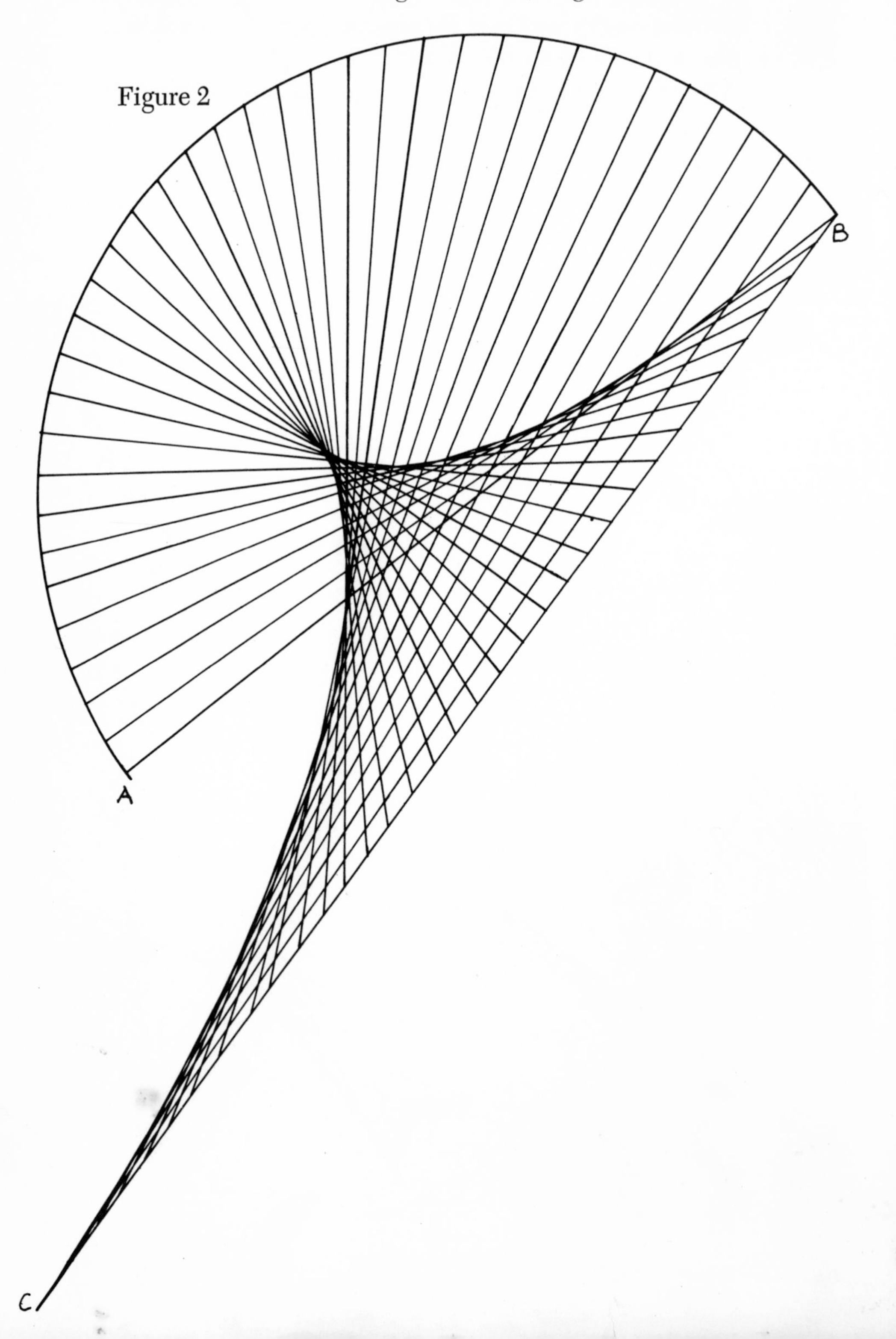

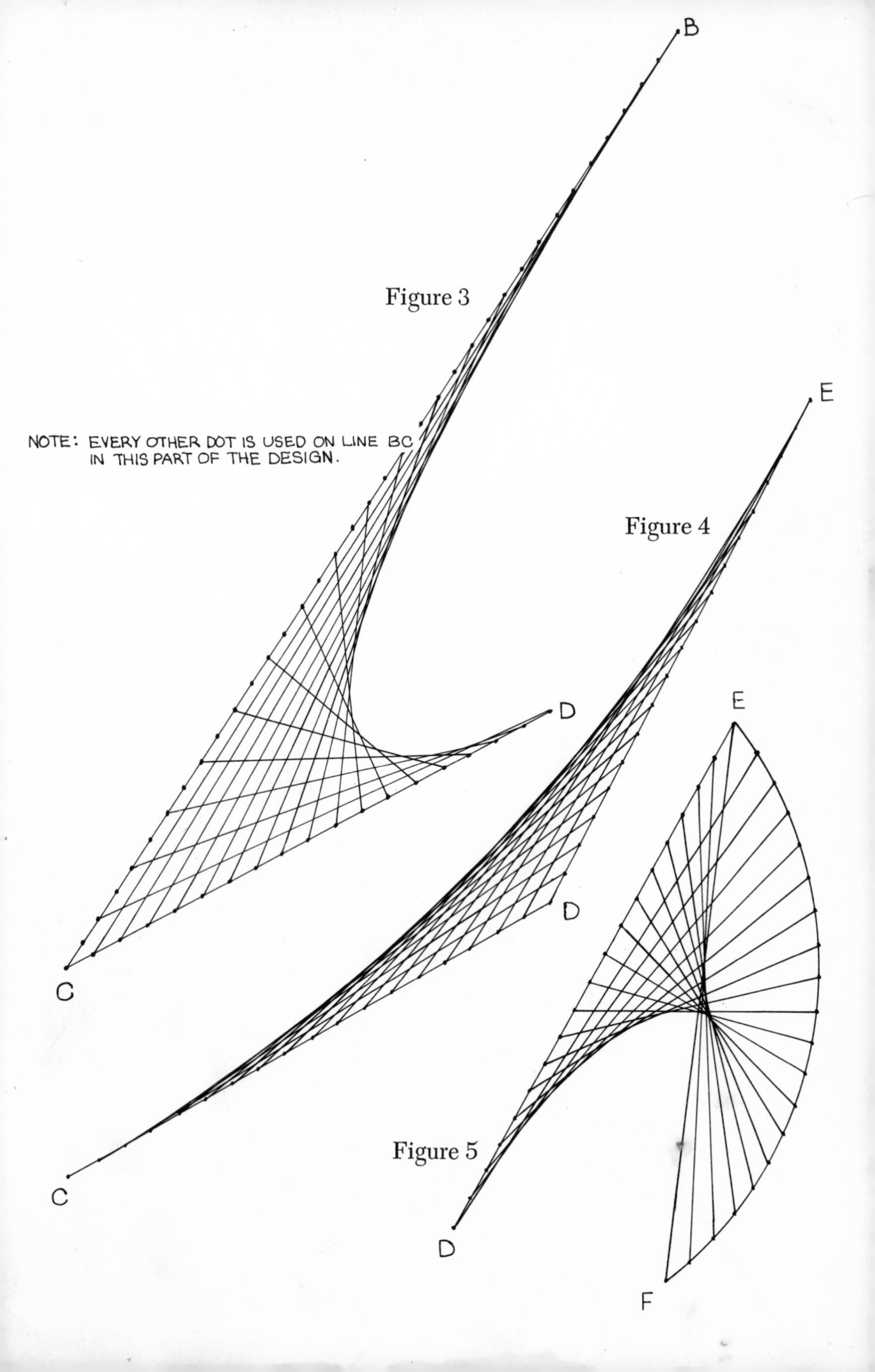

Figure 3
Figure 4
Figure 5

6. The completed design looks like Figure 6.

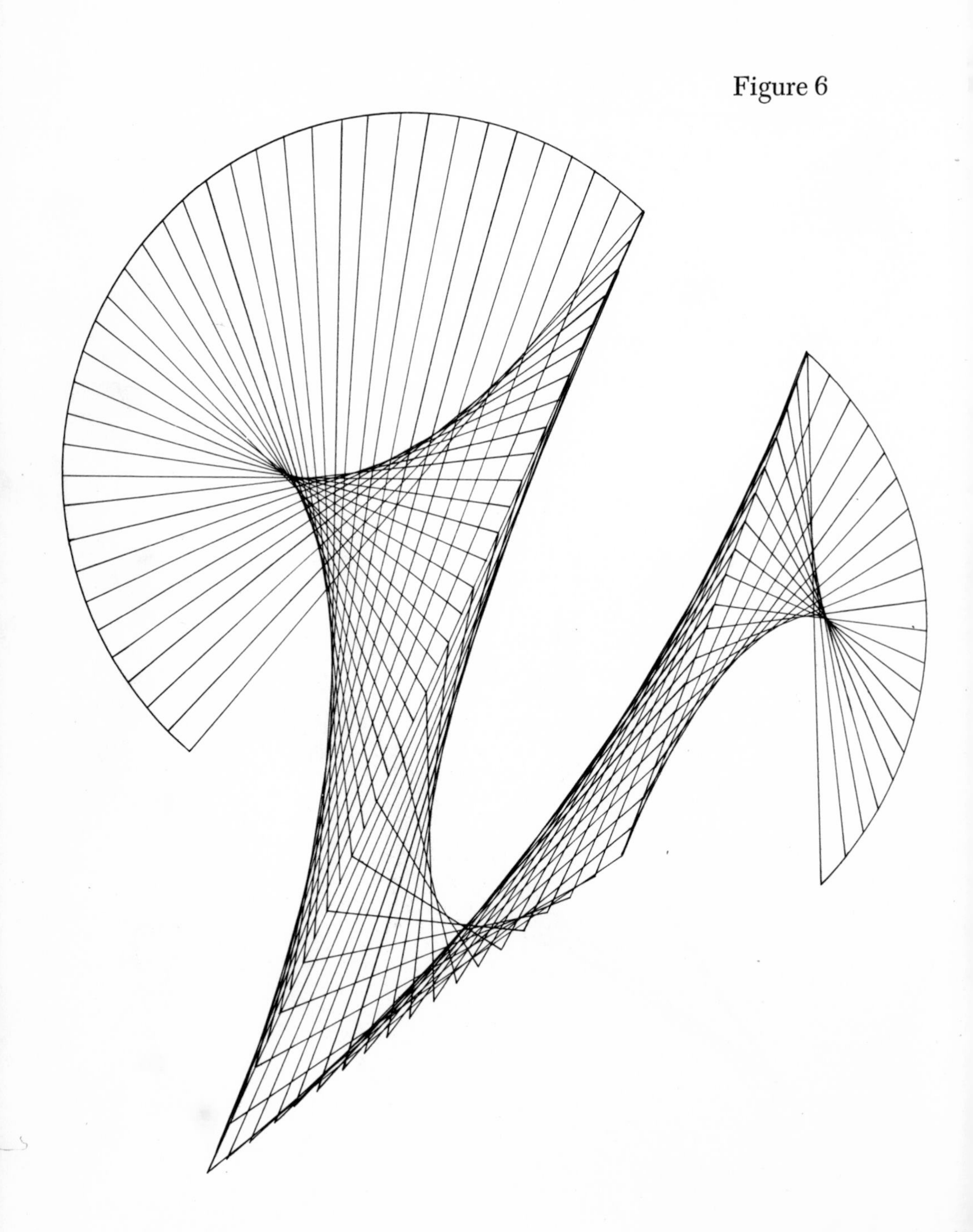

Figure 6

7. Take one part of a design already created and work new designs, like those on this page and the next page.

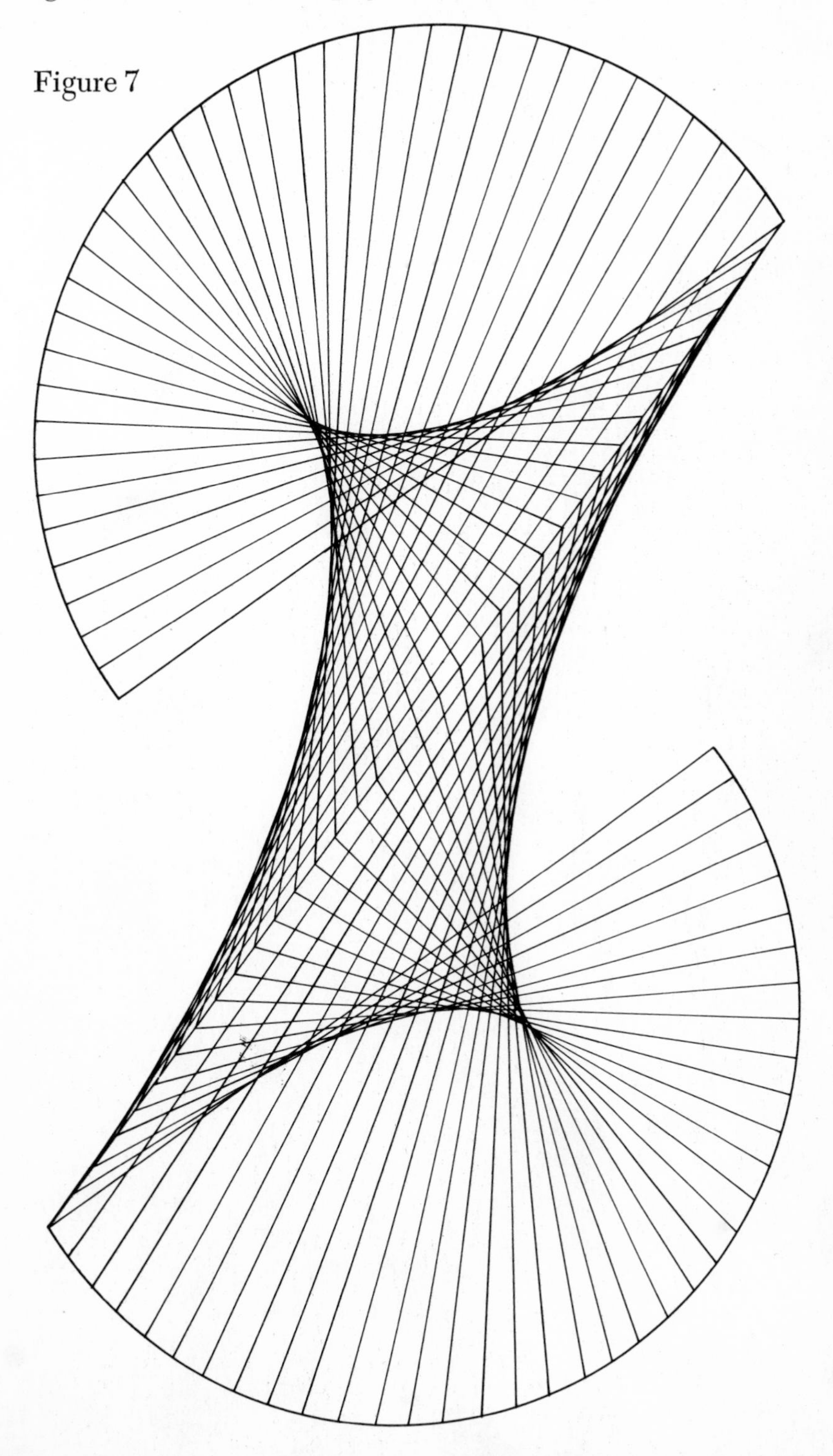

Figure 7

Figure 8

8. Here is one more example of a design made by combining angles and arcs.

Figure 9

Adding Color to Pencil Designs

Add color to your pencil designs by using colored threads or yarns. Add texture by using different sizes of threads or various weights and textures of yarn or both in the same design.

You will need:
Spools of different colored threads
Needles with eyes just large enough to thread easily
A thimble to fit your index finger
Lightweight cardboard
Scotch tape
Scissors

Sources of lightweight cardboard:
Ladies' hose packages
Men's shirt packages
Men's shirts back from the laundry
Lids and bottoms of shoe boxes or gift boxes
School supply stores—oak tag

To punch holes in lightweight cardboard:
1. Hold a sharp needle firmly between your thumb and middle finger. Use a thimble on your index finger to help push the needle through the cardboard. Keep the needle straight over the hole you are punching.
2. For heavier cardboard insert the eye part of a needle into the eraser end of a pencil, and punch as instructed in Step 1.
3. To prevent your cardboard from bending, put your hand under it to support it, but *spread your fingers where the punching takes place!*

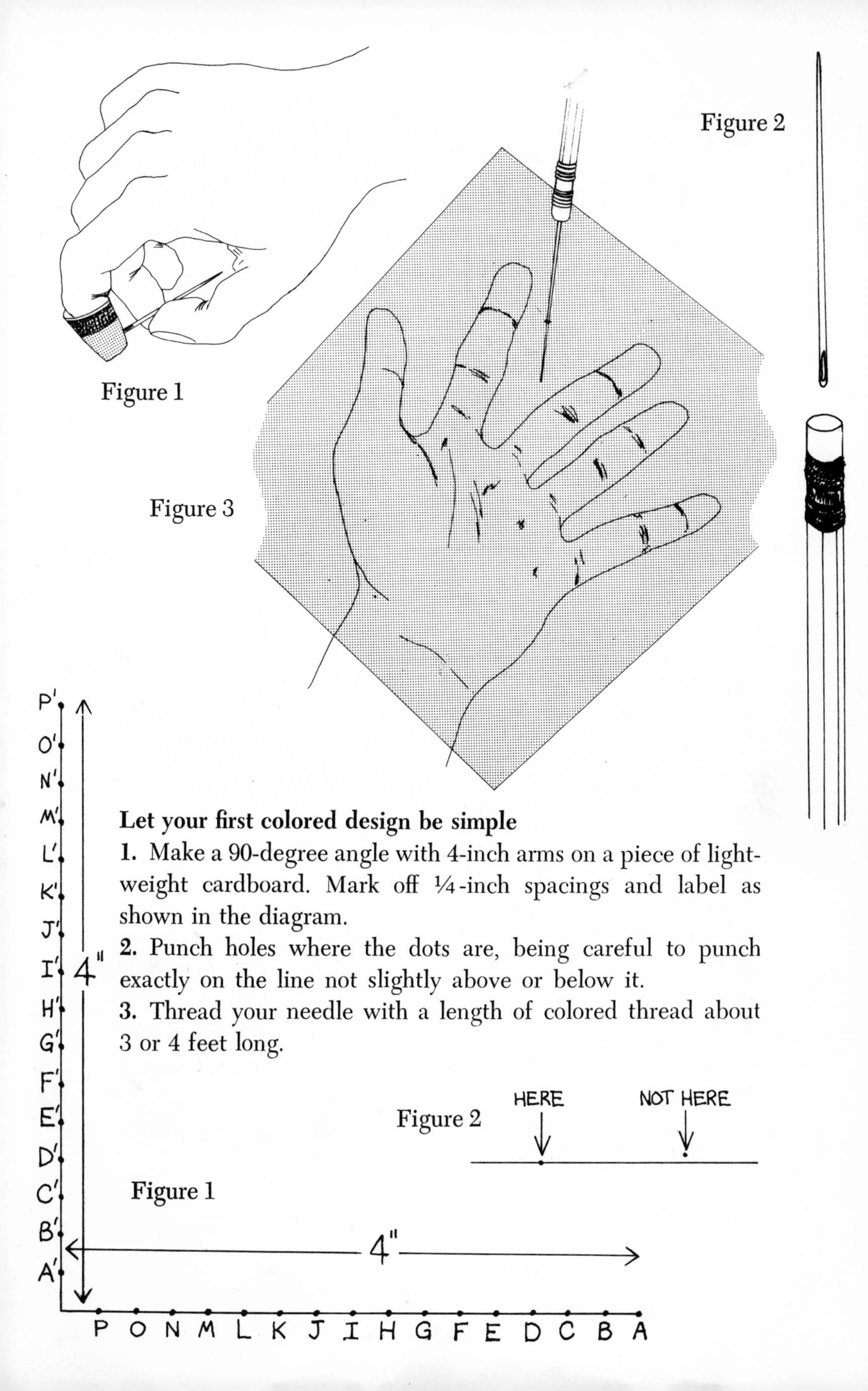

Figure 1

Figure 2

Figure 3

Let your first colored design be simple

1. Make a 90-degree angle with 4-inch arms on a piece of lightweight cardboard. Mark off ¼-inch spacings and label as shown in the diagram.

2. Punch holes where the dots are, being careful to punch exactly on the line not slightly above or below it.

3. Thread your needle with a length of colored thread about 3 or 4 feet long.

Figure 2

Figure 1

4. With your needle pierce through the back side of your design through the dot marked A in the diagram and pull the thread through until there is just 1 inch of thread showing on the back.
5. Fasten the thread securely with a small piece of Scotch tape; avoid covering the punched holes.
6. Go to the dot above the vertex (A^1 in diagram) and push your needle through from the front. As you pull your thread tight, your first straight line has been "drawn" in. If your thread tangles, don't jerk it. Using another needle, untangle the thread; then pull it tight.
7. Come up through dot B^1, and go down through dot B for your second straight line.
8. Up through dot C and down through dot C^1 produce the next one.
9. Continue until you have completed up through dot P^1 and down through dot P.
10. Pull the thread from the needle and anchor it with Scotch tape. Cut off any part of the thread that is over an inch long. If you start to run out of thread before your design is finished, tape it down on the *back*. With a new thread start at the hole next to the one where you taped the old thread, just as you would have continued had the thread not run out.

Go back now to your pencil designs and pick out one of your favorites.
1. Cut a piece of lightweight cardboard to fit your design.
2. Fasten the design to the cardboard so that when you start punching, the design won't slip. Use Scotch tape, letting it touch only the front of your pencil design and the back of your cardboard. Line up the top of the sheet with the design and the top of the cardboard.
3. Punch dots through both the design and the cardboard, holding your needle straight up and down.

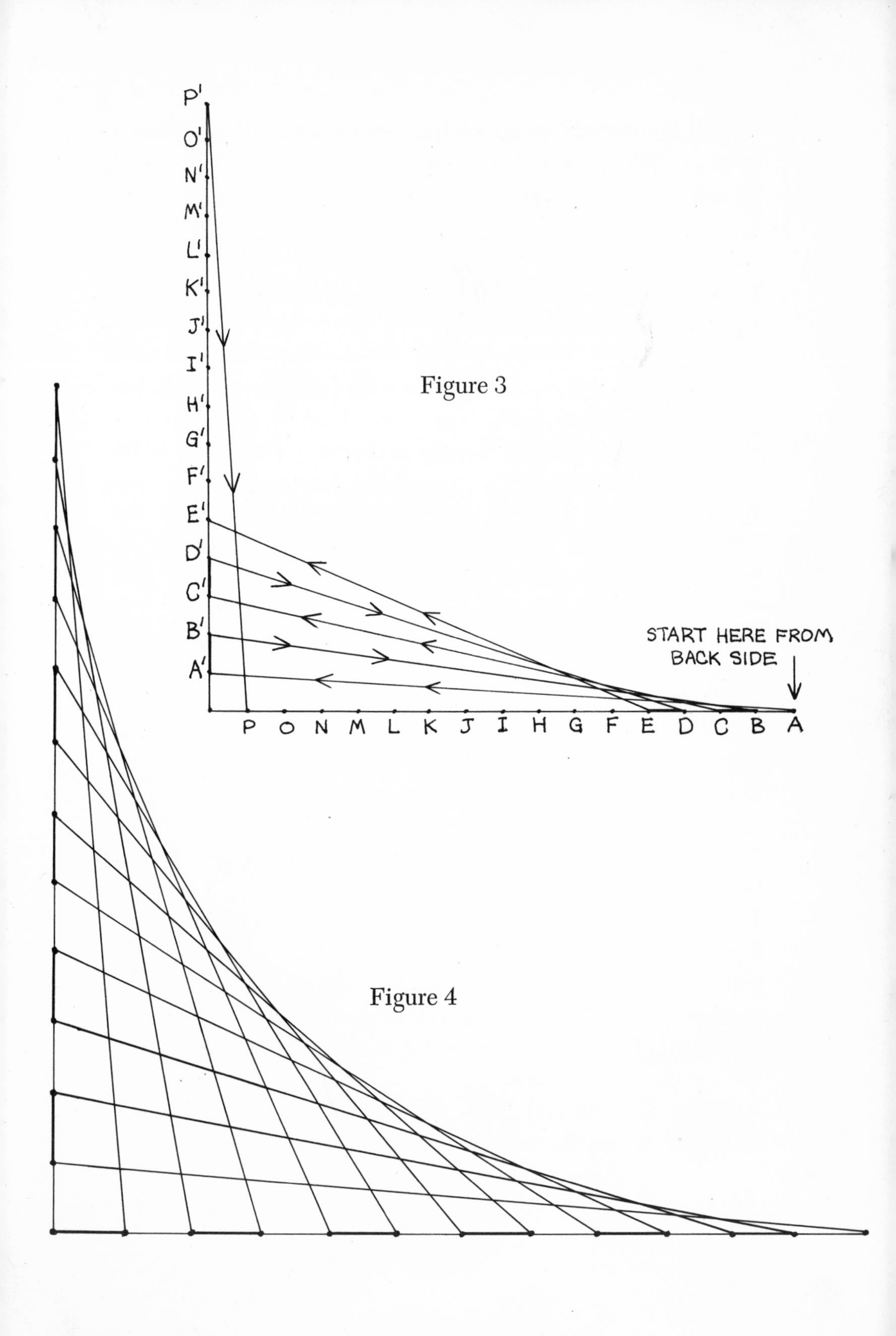

Figure 3

Figure 4

4. Remove the pencil design from the cardboard, and keep it in front of you while you work.
5. Select your thread. Use one color, different shades of the same color, or several colors. If your cardboard is white, select darker colors.
6. Work the design so that the colored lines are the same as the lines in your pencil design.

Save your pencil patterns. You can use them over and over, experimenting with new designs or color combinations. You can combine two designs. You can make a set by reversing your pattern the second time, turning it over to punch holes in the cardboard, and using the same color combinations on both designs.

When you have finished some particularly interesting designs, you might want to frame them.

Doing Your Own Thing

You now have all the basic rules for designing. Begin experimenting with new designs by putting one design over another; by putting a curved line or two over a design; by working with parallel lines; by backing one design up against another; or any other way you can think of.

When putting one design over another, try using different textures of thread, such as bouclés, or crochet threads, or different weights of yarn. Try any of the variegated threads for unusual color blending. Use double strands of regular thread or one of the textures just mentioned on one pattern and single strands of thread on another. If you use the same kind of thread on both patterns, try using a brighter color on the first design so that it will show through after you have put the second design over it.

Using Colored Background

Try mounting a piece of colored construction paper over your cardboard before laying your pencil design on.

1. Anchor the colored paper at the corners with a small amount of Scotch tape.

2. Put your design on and anchor it as you did before, letting the tape touch only the front of your design and the back of the cardboard.

3. When you have finished punching the holes, remove only the pencil design.

4. If you have chosen a dark sheet of colored paper, use lighter colors of thread. Try white or any of the pastels on a royal blue, or black, or deep purple, or magenta background.

If you find that your punching is getting more difficult with the addition of construction paper, you might invest in a small beaverboard bulletin board. (Stationery counters in department stores or lumber companies often carry them.) After you have taped your construction paper to your cardboard, anchor them and the pencil design to the beaverboard with thumb tacks. Punch your holes, remove the tacks, and proceed as before.

Fabric Backgrounds

Another background you might want to use is a loosely woven, solid-colored material mounted on cardboard. In mounting, keep the weave of the cloth straight, not on a bias (slant). There are several ways to anchor the cloth to the cardboard.

Tape it as you did the colored construction paper. Cut the material the same size as the cardboard, but anchor it all along the edges with Scotch tape rather than just at the corners.

You could anchor the cloth by stitching it all around the edges, in which case begin as suggested in the preceding paragraph. Stitch it by hand (a running stitch, just up and down through the cardboard all the way around) or with a sewing machine set at the longest stitch.

Another method is to anchor it on the back with either Scotch tape or a good glue.

1. Cut the material 2 inches longer and 2 inches wider than the cardboard.

2. Place the material on a flat surface so that the side you want to show in the finished design is down.

3. Put the cardboard on top of the material so that 1-inch of cloth extends all the way around the cardboard.

4. Place a small amount of glue on each corner of the cardboard and turn each corner of the cloth over the cardboard corner so that it makes a neat triangle (see the diagram).

5. When the corners have dried, put glue all along the outer edge of the cardboard (not more than 1-inch wide) and press the material onto it. Don't pull the material.

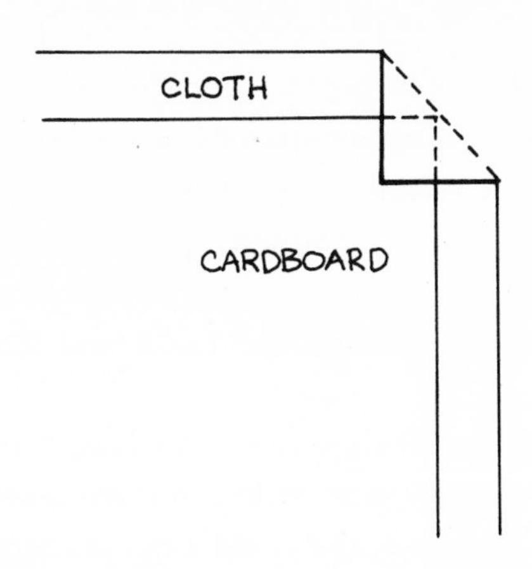

6. When your cloth background is thoroughly dry, put your paper design over it and anchor it securely with Scotch tape. Use thin paper for your design.
7. Punch holes through the pattern, the material, and the cardboard. When you have finished, *leave the pencil pattern on the background.*
8. Work your design over the pencil pattern; then tear the pattern very carefully from under the thread.

Corrugated Cardboard
Want something entirely different? Use a piece of corrugated board, the kind packing boxes are made of.
1. Cut a large piece from one side.
2. Make your design large, putting your dots farther apart but keeping them evenly spaced.
3. Anchor your design at the corners onto the cardboard with thumb tacks, and punch the holes.
4. Remove the pencil design. Put thumb tacks, very small pins, or carpet tacks into the punched holes. Dip the tips into glue first so that they will stay firmly in position.
5. Instead of sewing your thread through the cardboard, work on the top side only, going around the tacks. The little threads that had always been on the back of the cardboard now show on the front.

Bulletin Board

A design on corrugated cardboard is very fragile and can easily be ruined by brushing against it. For a sturdier design, a bulletin board, already framed, can be used instead. Thumb tacks hold well. Proceed with the design as above. When you tire of the design, remove the tacks and thread and make a new design.

For a permanent design, use a flat board and hammer carpet tacks or small nails into it after you have marked the places for the holes. Proceed as you did with the corrugated board. Painting the board before putting the pattern on will add color to the finished product.

Have a wonderful time creating and working your designs! Maybe it will lead into a very interesting and useful hobby.

Index

italics indicate illustration

About the Author

Elsie C. Ellison, who taught school for many years, devised the scheme for *Fun With Lines and Curves* as a unit for one of her math classes at the Wilson Hill School in Worthington, Ohio. An instant success, the activity intrigued both the children and their parents, who urged Mrs. Ellison to write a book about it.

Mrs. Ellison was born in Middletown, Ohio, and attended public schools there. Later, she received B. S. and M. E. degrees from Miami University in Oxford, Ohio, and did additional work at the Ohio State University and the University of Florida in Gainesville. Mrs. Ellison and her husband live in Treasure Island, Florida.